President of Queens College

Report of President of Queen's College

Belfast, 1898-99

President of Queens College

Report of President of Queen's College
Belfast, 1898-99

ISBN/EAN: 9783742800077

Manufactured in Europe, USA, Canada, Australia, Japa

Cover: Foto ©Thomas Meinert / pixelio.de

Manufactured and distributed by brebook publishing software
(www.brebook.com)

President of Queens College

Report of President of Queen's College

THE REPORT

OF THE

PRESIDENT

OF

QUEEN'S COLLEGE, BELFAST,

FOR

THE YEAR 1898-99.

Presented to both Houses of Parliament by Command of Her Majesty.

DUBLIN:
PRINTED FOR HER MAJESTY'S STATIONERY OFFICE,
BY ALEXANDER THOM & CO. (LIMITED).

And to be purchased, either directly or through any Bookseller, from
HODGES, FIGGIS & Co. (LIMITED), 104, Grafton-street, Dublin; or
EYRE AND SPOTTISWOODE, East Harding-street, Fleet-street, E.C., and
32, Abingdon-street, Westminster, S.W.; or
JOHN MENZIES & Co., 12, Hanover-street, Edinburgh, and
90, West Nile-street, Glasgow.

1899.

THE REPORT

OF THE

PRESIDENT OF QUEEN'S COLLEGE, BELFAST.

FOR THE

YEAR 1898-99.

TO THE QUEEN'S MOST EXCELLENT MAJESTY.

MAY IT PLEASE YOUR MAJESTY,

I have the honour to present to Your Majesty my annual Report on the condition and progress of Queen's College, Belfast, during the academic year 1898-99. I am happy to be able to say that the College continues to prosecute, with unabated vigour and no small measure of success, the high task committed to it by Your Majesty. I proceed to speak in detail of the various departments of its work.

LECTURES.

According to the statutes of the College our First Term commences on the third Tuesday in the month of October in each year, and of late we have endeavoured to begin lectures at the earliest possible date after that day. In point of fact they now commence much sooner than was formerly the case. The Degree Examinations of the Royal University, to which the majority of our students resort, are just concluding towards the end of October, and our own examinations for Matriculation, Scholarships, and Studentships overlap them, and occupy the first week and more of the Term. Notwithstanding, lectures began last autumn on October 18th, so that when the First Term ended at Christmas a very substantial amount of work had been accomplished in the various class-rooms. When it is borne in mind that, since the institution of our Summer Session, certain of our classes continue to meet until towards the end of the month of July, it will be evident that our academic year is not deficient in length, and it is also to be remembered that no small part of the Long Vacation is occupied by professors and students in University Examinations, which to both constitute part of their severest and most trying work.

The attendance of students at lectures has been, I am happy to say, of the most regular and satisfactory character. A short time ago the Council made certain alterations in the requirements regarding attendance, and during the Session now under review, whether owing to these changes or not, the attendance was the best which we have had for a long time. I have also once more the satisfaction of reporting to Your Majesty that the conduct and demeanour of the students generally was everything that could be desired. No breach of College discipline was brought under the notice of the Council during the year.

Honours Gained during the Year.

The assiduity with which the studies of the College were prosecuted during the year is illustrated by the list of successful competitors for our Studentships, Scholarships, and Prizes, for the Degrees and Honours of the Royal University, the University of Oxford, and the University of Cambridge and at the various examinations of the Temple and King's Inns, which will be found appended to this Report.

At our own examinations the competition was, as usual, keen and vigorous. We always note with interest the Ulster schools whose pupils distinguish themselves at our examinations for Entrance Scholarships in Arts, for we recognise the dependence of the College upon the schools. The first place in the list of Literary Scholars last autumn was gained by Mr. Phineas M'Kee, of the Royal Academical Institution, Belfast; and the first place in the list of Science Scholars by Mr. William Hawthorne, of the Upper Sullivan School, Holywood. Scholarships were also won by pupils of the Methodist College, Belfast; the Academical Institution, Coleraine; and the Intermediate School, Moneymore. The lists were notable from the fact that the very unusual number of three gentlemen gained double Scholarships, viz.:—Mr. Phineas M'Kee and Mr. Edward James Hagan, of the Royal Academical Institution, Belfast, and Mr. Robert Martin Houston, of the Academical Institution, Coleraine. Another significant feature of our Scholarship Examinations last Session was the number of young ladies who took high places at them. Miss Sarah Robena Beatty Smiley succeeded in gaining second place on the list of First Year Literary Scholars; Miss Margaret Stouppe won a Second Year Literary Scholarship, and Miss Mary Elizabeth Clements a Second Year Scholarship in Law. In the Class Prize Lists I was also glad to see the names of several young ladies occupying honourable positions. The alteration recently introduced into our Statutes, which gives to women exactly the same privileges as men in the competitions for Scholarships and other prizes, was evidently not made in vain.

At the various examinations outside our own walls at which our students competed, many of them acquitted themselves with signal success. Full lists of these will be found in the Appendix; here I can only refer to them in the briefest and most general manner. At the Summer Examinations of the Royal University last year this College topped the Honours List with a total of 64 honours and exhibitions (viz., 18 first honours, 28 second, and 18 exhibitions), being first by a long way among all the colleges of Ireland. (I exclude of course in this statement honours gained at Matriculation). At the Autumn Examinations of the same University the results were not dissimilar in point of numbers, and they included such signal distinctions as the Junior Fellowship in Mathematical Science gained by Mr. W. A. Houston, the University Studentship in Ancient Classics won by Mr. R. M. Henry, and the Medical Studentship gained by Dr. Thomas Houston—a truly remarkable trinity of honours. At the Spring Medical Examinations of the present year the Belfast students carried off all the honours and exhibitions which were awarded, with one exception, including a First Class Exhibition with the Degree of M.B., which was gained by Mr. J. W. D. Megaw. An unbroken record such as this requires no comment. It is as honourable to the professors as to the students.

At other seats of learning the results during the year have been much the same. At King's Inns ten candidates entered for the highest honour open to students for the Irish Bar—the John Brooke Scholarship. It was gained by Mr. Robert Spencer Park, this being the seventh occasion in eight years on which an *alumnus* of this College carried off this coveted prize. Whilst the first place at the Irish Law Examinations was thus won by a Belfast-man, it is significant that the corresponding place in England was also taken by another of our students—Mr. W. J. Purvis—who gained the Studentship of the Council of Legal Education. Only a few of the other notable positions achieved during the year can I mention. Mr. J. G. Leathem, a Fellow of St. John's College, Cambridge, was appointed Lecturer in Mathematics in that College. Mr. A. Fraser Everett gained at New College, Oxford, the History Exhibition of £50 per annum tenable during residence, and in the Final Honours School of Jurisprudence of the University of Oxford Mr. J. Stewart Wallace was awarded First Class Honours. Mr. Benjamin Moore, the first student whom we nominated eight years ago to one of the newly instituted Research Scholarships established by Her Majesty's Commissioners of the Exhibition of 1851, has been appointed Professor of Physiology in Yale University. Dr. William Hanna has been appointed by the Government Special Plague Medical Officer in Madras, and more recently has been transferred, at the request of the Government of Bombay, to the Government Laboratory in Bombay. Mr. T. R. Collier has been appointed to the Principalship of the Royal Academy, Belfast, and Mr. James Cowan to that of Lurgan College. And while this Report is passing through the press I learn with sincere pleasure that Mr. J. Sinclair Baxter has gained by competitive examination the Reid Professorship of Constitutional and Criminal Law in the University of Dublin, while the candidate who took second place at the examination, also one of our *alumni*, Mr. R. R. M'Cutcheon, made such distinguished answering that he was awarded a special prize of £40.

During the year we had the pleasure of nominating Mr. William Caldwell, B.A., to a Research Scholarship of Her Majesty's Commissioners of the Exhibition of 1851; Dr. Henry Stewart Anderson to a commission in the Royal Army Medical Corps; and Dr. H. Norman Barnett and Dr. Alexander E. Knight to Civil Surgeonships in attendance on Her Majesty's troops.

The Chair of English Law.

In December last, to the general regret of the entire College, Professor James Andrew Strahan found it necessary, owing to the increase of his professional work in London, to place in my hands his resignation of the Chair of English Law, which he had held for thirteen years, having been appointed by Your Majesty in 1886. During all that time our Law School enjoyed very gratifying prosperity and achieved singular success, as my annual reports have testified from year to year, and of this success Mr. Strahan might truly say—*pars magna fui*. Not only, moreover, did he devote himself with conspicuous ability and unflagging zeal to the work of his Chair, but he also threw his energies into the entire life of the College, and was always one of the foremost in assisting every movement for the advancement of its interests. Along with Sir Wm. MacCormac, President of the Royal College of Surgeons, he was one of the founders of the "Association of Old Belfastmen, London," which has done and continues to do so much for the promotion of a very desirable *esprit de corps* among former students of the College resident in England. He was also one of the earliest and warmest friends of our Union, which has proved such a valuable factor in promoting the comfort and well-being of the students, and in many other ways he uniformly exhibited a deep interest in the welfare of his *Alma Mater* and a laudable energy in advancing it. On his retirement his friends and former pupils testified their regard for him and their sincere regret at his departure by entertaining him at a public dinner in Belfast.

The Chair left vacant by the retirement of Professor Strahan was conferred by Your Majesty on Mr. W. Newell Watts, LL.D., an *alumnus* and ex-Scholar of the College like his predecessor, a brilliant honourman of the Middle Temple and King's Inns, and a member both of the Irish and English Bars.

New Department.

Last year we received a communication from the Secretary of State for the Colonies (the Right Hon. Joseph Chamberlain, M.P.), suggesting for our consideration the advisability of establishing a special department for giving instruction in the diseases of tropical countries to such students of medicine as contemplated entering the colonial service of the State. After careful consideration and inquiry, the College Council came to the conclusion that it was our duty to do everything in our power to further an object so laudable, and accordingly an application was made to His Excellency the Lord Lieutenant of Ireland for permission to appoint a Lecturer on Tropical Diseases. Our request was granted, and we hope that in the near future this new Lectureship will be in operation. In addition to serving the special purpose primarily intended to be met by its establishment, it will have the additional advantage of affording to such of our students as intend becoming Medical Missionaries an opportunity of familiarising themselves with the diagnosis and recognised treatment of tropical diseases, and already a large proportion of the ladies and gentlemen who are studying medicine here, with the view of becoming foreign missionaries, have expressed their intention of taking advantage of the proposed lectures. This new department is the sixth which has been established in the College within the last seven years.

The Work of the Deans of Residences.

I have received the following reports from the Deans of Residences, whose disinterested and self-denying attention to the moral and religious welfare of the students belonging to their respective communions is deserving of hearty recognition. I give the reports in the order of seniority of the Deans:—

"St. Andrew's Rectory,
"University Square,
"Belfast, June 5, 1899.

"Dear Mr. President,—I have much pleasure in presenting my report, as Church Dean of Residences, for the past Session. In general, I may remark that the progress of the students in their habits and deportment is most gratifying. There is a tone amongst them that cannot but be pleasing to all lovers of their well-being. Very much of this is due to the work of the Christian Union, which has been earnestly and successfully carried out throughout the Session. In December last the Session was inaugurated by a social meeting of the students, carried out by the Union, with the help and supervision of the Deans of Residences. Then followed meetings, such as Bible Circles, missionary meetings, lady members' religious meetings, and the like. The result has been a stimulus to the study of spiritual truths, faith, and life, which has manifested itself in the progress above referred to. I have therefore once again to say that the conduct of the students has been most exemplary.

"I remain, dear Mr. President,
"Your faithful Servant,
"S. Edward Busby, Clk., M.A., LL.D., T.C.D.,
"Dean (I.C.), Q.C.B.

"The Rev. the President, D.D.,
"Queen's College, Belfast."

———

"College Park, Belfast,
"13th June, 1899.

"Dear Sir,—I have had but little opportunity of meeting with the students of Queen's College during the Session, owing chiefly to the difficulty of arranging for a stated hour of meeting in the College. At the beginning of the Session I saw many of them at a social meeting in connexion with the College Christian Union, to which all the students of the first year were personally invited.

"The College Christian Union has this Session seventy-five members, and meetings for prayer and for the study of the Bible have been held regularly by the students during the Session.

"As far as known to me, the conduct and character of all the students belonging to the Presbyterian Church have been exceedingly good; and many of them are earnest Christian men, who exercise a healthy religious and moral influence in the College.

"I am,

"Yours faithfully,

"Matthew Leitch,

"Dean of Residences for Students belonging "to the Presbyterian Church."

"Methodist College, Belfast,
"12th June, 1899.

"Dear Mr. President,—I have reason to believe that the students under my care, as Methodist Dean of Residences, have conducted themselves in every respect without reproach.

"Yours very truly,

"Wm. Nicholas, D.D.

"To the President,
"Queen's College, Belfast."

"Adelaide Park, Belfast,
"June 1, 1899.

"Dear Sir,—It gives me pleasure to say that I can report favourably of the students who have been under my care during the past Session of the College.

"Yours faithfully,

"Douglas Walmsley.

"To the President,
"Queen's College, Belfast."

The College Buildings

have not only been well maintained during the year, but several important structural improvements have been carried out. Some of these are elsewhere referred to, and, amongst others, I may mention that the Entrance Hall has been paved with marble and effectively heated by means of radiators; the North Cloister has been flagged; a convenient Ladies' Room has been provided and fitted up, and important improvements in the lighting and heating of several of the rooms in the Anatomical Department have been carried out.

The College Library.

During the year the Library Committee, consisting of Professors Dougan, Morton, Park, Cunningham, Symington, Thompson, Cuming, Byers, the Librarian (Dr. Meissner), and myself, met regularly, and did much useful work. Mr. William Rapple was appointed Assistant Librarian, in the room of Mr. William Taylor, whose resignation (after nearly twenty years' faithful service), I regretfully reported last year, and who has since died. The daily closing hour of the Library was altered to 4 o'clock p.m., instead of 3, on Mondays, Tuesdays, Wednesdays, Thursdays, and Fridays, and 1 o'clock on Saturdays, instead of 12. The close season was also much abbreviated. These changes will, I feel sure, contribute to the convenience and advantage of readers.

The number of works added to the Library, during the year, was 757—viz., 484 volumes and 273 other publications. Most of these were purchased, but for a considerable number we were indebted to the thoughtful kindness of *alumni* and other friends. The donations will be found fully acknowledged in an Appendix to this Report. The Library is now estimated to contain about 65,000 volumes.

The Museums.

The various Museums were sedulously cared for during the year.

The capacity of the Natural History Museum was considerably increased by the erection of a new gallery, fitted with wall cases. Much-needed accommodation has, in this way, been afforded for specimens hitherto either unexhibited, or crowded miscellaneously together. Several important presentations were made to this Museum. Among these may be mentioned one by Mr. Henry Hanna, M.A., B.SC., a former student of the College who is now Demonstrator of Botany and Palæontology in the Royal College of Science, Dublin, and who contributed through Professor Cunningham a collection of interesting botanical specimens. Various other additions were obtained by purchase.

The onerous but important work of re-arranging and cataloguing the Medical Museum, to which I referred in last year's Report, has made further progress during the year under the zealous supervision of the Curator, Professor Symington, and with the valuable and willing assistance of several young medical men and a lady medical student. Several useful type-collections of fractures, &c. are being formed, and additional cases and shelving are being provided. The Council showed their sense of the value of the work which is being done by making during the winter a special grant of £50 towards the further equipment of this Museum, which, I am informed, contains one of the most complete collections to be found in the Kingdom. It has received many valuable donations, which will be found duly acknowledged in the Appendix, and for which we heartily thank the donors.

In my last Report I had the pleasure of announcing a kindly and unsolicited donation of £20 which I had received from "Two Friends," for the purpose of commencing a fund for the establishment of a Museum of Hygiene or Sanitary Science. Referring to it I said, "Such an institution will, when opened, not only prove most valuable to the Department of Sanitary Science, which Dr. Letts and Dr. Whitaker are assiduously labouring to develop, but will, I hope, render essential service to the health of the entire community in which our lot is cast." I am now happy to report that this new Museum is an accomplished fact. A large room has been provided for receiving its exhibits, and this is being fitted up for their accommodation. Not a few valuable donations of specimens and models (a full list of which, with the names of their donors, will be given later on), have been contributed to it by gentlemen who recognise the value and usefulness of such a Museum, and some important purchases have been made. It is only right that I should add that the inception and success of this Museum are largely due to the enlightened zeal and untiring energy of Dr. Henry O'Neill, of this city, who has spared no pains and grudges no time to its establishment and equipment. The Council has appointed him Honorary Curator of the Museum, which will always be associated with his name, and which, as years roll on, will, I trust, be found of increasing value to the College and the city. I sincerely hope that it will continue to receive the practical sympathy and help of the public. From the same "Two Friends" I have received a further generous and unasked donation, to form the nucleus of a fund for adding to the equipment of the various scientific departments of the College. All of these are in deep need of such kindly and considerate help, as the funds at our disposal for the purchase of apparatus, &c., are very far from sufficient, and it is unnecessary for me to say that I should be sincerely glad if other thoughtful friends of education would follow the excellent example thus set.

The Union.

The Union has had, I am glad to say, another prosperous and useful Session, and continues to fulfil the high promise of its early days. Its reading rooms, debating hall, dining room, and recreation rooms are largely frequented by graduates and undergraduates. Last winter a library was established, for which handsome and capacious book-cases have been provided. These already contain a considerable number of volumes, and I hope the collection will be increased by many donations, in addition to such books as may be purchased. I have received and read with interest the annual report and statement of accounts of the Union, issued by its Committee, and I am glad to know that last winter showed a pleasant addition to the roll of membership, and that its affairs continue to be managed with commendable ability and success. Open, as the Union is, to all *alumni* and students of the College, at a very small fee, and affording, as it does, most valuable advantages, I trust that not only will students in actual attendance seek to connect themselves with it, but that more and more of our graduates will associate themselves by means of it with the present generation of college men. Mr. J. R. Gillespie, M.A., was President during last Session. Mr. John M'Crea, B.A., has been elected his successor.

I cannot pass from the subject of the Union without referring to a presentation which was made last winter to its accomplished architect, Mr. Robert Cochrane, F.R.I.B.A., F.S.A., to whose skill and labour its buildings owe their beauty and commodiousness. The Executive Committee felt that they could not allow their very pleasant connection with him to come to an end without, in some tangible form, expressing their sense of the valuable services which he had rendered to the Union without fee or reward, not only by the admirable plans which he prepared for the building, and the unremitting attention which he gave to its erection, but for the sympathetic interest which he took in the project from its inception. Accordingly, they asked and obtained permission to present him with a drawingroom clock, suitably inscribed, and this, in accordance with his wishes, was handed to him without any public formality, along with a letter expressive of their feelings. The pleasure of our connection with Mr. Cochrane was increased by our knowledge that he is an old Queensman, a fact which doubtless contributed to his hearty interest in the establishment of the Union. I must add that the entire College has benefited materially by his appointment to the Surveyorship of the Northern District of Ireland, in which the College is situated, and of whose buildings he is therefore in charge. We owe much to the wise care and active interest of the Board of Works, who have the good fortune to have him as one of their chief officers, and I feel it due alike to them and to him to make this public acknowledgment of our obligations.

The College Societies.

The several College Societies, which the students have formed amongst themselves for their improvement and pleasure, held most of their meetings during the Session, some of which were of more than ordinary interest, in the M'Mordie Hall of the Union. At the opening meeting of the Literary and Scientific Society, which has now completed the fiftieth year of its history, the new President (Mr. O. R. Reid, B.A.) read his inaugural paper, and the Lord Chief Justice of Ireland (Sir Peter O'Brien, Bart.), delivered a much appreciated address. At another of its meetings Mr. F. R. Benson favoured the members with a very interesting lecture on "Art and Athletics," and at a third, the Right Hon. Horace Plunkett, M.P. discussed, with characteristic force and lucidity, the development of the material resources of Ireland, a subject which he has made so thoroughly his own, and in connection with which he has rendered such undoubted and valuable service to the country. In addition to these public assemblages of the Society there was the usual full complement of private meetings, at which the members debated various subjects among themselves. The Medical Students' Association had also a prosperous and useful session under the presidency of Mr. W. A. Rice, B.A. Various topics of professional interest were discussed at its meetings.

I have thus endeavoured to tell the round unvarnished tale of the history of the College during the academic year now completed. Full statistics will be found in the Appendix to this Report, in which I have placed lists of the Visitors and other Officials of the College, together with a series of tables showing (1) the Number of Students matriculated in the Session 1898-99; (2) the Numbers and Religious Persuasions of the Students who have entered in each year since the opening of the College, and the Numbers and Religious Persuasions of the Students who have attended in each year; (3) the Numbers attending in each Faculty during the Session now ended; (4) the Number of Students who came to the College from each of the provinces of Ireland, and from other places, during the Session; (5) the Ages of the Students in attendance; (6) the Number of Lectures given by each Professor during the Session, and the Number of Students attending each Class; (7) the names of the College Scholars and Prizemen for last Session; (8) a list of Degrees, Diplomas, and Honours obtained by Students of the College at the Examinations of the Royal University of Ireland in 1898; (9) a list of sundry Students who have obtained distinctions in Universities other than the Royal University of Ireland; (10) a Table showing the Length of Service, Salaries, and other Emoluments of the Professors and Officers of the College; (11) a list of the Benefactors of the College since its foundation, with an account of their Benefactions; and (12) an account of the Receipts and Expenditure of the College during the year ending 31st March, 1899.

All which is testified on behalf of the College by

Your Majesty's

Most dutiful servant,

THOMAS HAMILTON,

PRESIDENT.

July, 1899.

VISITORS.

The Most Honourable the Marquess of Dufferin and Ava, K.P., G.C.B.

The Most Honourable the Marquess of Londonderry, K.G.

The Right Honourable A. M. Porter, Master of the Rolls in Ireland.

His Honour Judge Shaw, Q.C.

The Right Rev. Bishop Welland, D.D.

The Right Honourable Thomas Sinclair, J.P., D.L.

The Right Honourable the Chief Secretary for Ireland, for the time being.

The Moderator of the General Assembly of the Presbyterian Church in Ireland, for the time being.

The President of the Royal College of Physicians, Ireland, for the time being.

The President of the Royal College of Surgeons, Ireland, for the time being.

The President of the Association of Non-Subscribing Presbyterians of Ireland for the time being.

PRESIDENT, PROFESSORS, &c., AND DEANS OF RESIDENCES

President.—The Rev. Thomas Hamilton, M.A., D.D., LL.D.

Professors.

The Greek Language,	Samuel Dill, M.A.
The Latin Language,	Thomas Wilson Dougan, M.A.
Mathematics,	John Purser, LL.D., D.Sc., F.R.U.I.
Natural Philosophy,	William Blair Morton, M.A., F.R.U.I.
History and English Literature,	Samuel James MacMullan, M.A., F.R.U.I.
Logic and Metaphysics,	John Park, M.A., D.Lit., F.R.U.I.
Chemistry,	Edmund Albert Letts, Ph.D., D.Sc., F.R.S.E., F.C.S., F.R.U.I.
Natural History and Geology,	Robert O. Cunningham, M.D., D.Sc., F.L.S., F.G.S., C.M.Z.S., F.R.U.I.
Modern Languages,	Albert Ludwig Meissner, Ph.D.
Jurisprudence & Political Economy,	William Graham, M.A.
English Law,	William Newell Watts, LL.D.
Anatomy,	Johnson Symington, M.D., F.R.S.E., F.R.U.I.
Dunville Chair of Physiology,	William Henry Thompson, M.D., F.R.C.S., Eng.
Medicine,	James Cuming, M.A., M.D., F.R.C.P.I.
Surgery,	Thomas Sinclair, M.D., M.Ch., F.R.C.S., Eng.
Materia Medica,	William Whitla, M.A., M.D.
Midwifery,	John William Byers, M.A., M.D., M.Ch., M.A.O.
Civil Engineering,	Maurice Frederick FitzGerald, B.A., Assoc. M.I.C.E.
Agriculture,	John Fred. Hodges, M.D., F.C.S., F.I.C.

Lecturers.

Medical Jurisprudence,	John Fred. Hodges, M.D., F.C.S., F.I.C.
Pathology,	James Lorrain Smith, M.A., M.D.
Ophthalmology and Otology,	William Alexander M'Keown, M.D.
Sanitary Science,	Edmund Albert Letts, Ph.D., D.Sc., F.R.S.E., F.C.S., F.R.U.I.; Henry Whitaker, M.D.

Demonstrator.

Practical Pharmacy,	Victor George L. Fielden, M.B.

Office Bearers.

Registrar,	John Purser, LL.D.
Bursar,	William Wylie.
Librarian,	Albert Ludwig Meissner, Ph.D.

Curator of Natural History Museum.—Professor Cunningham, M.D.

Curator of Medical Museum.—Professor Symington, M.D.

Hon. Curator of Sanitary Science Museum.—Henry O'Neill, M.D., M.Ch.

Deans of Residences.

		Appointed
Church of Ireland,	Rev. S. Edward Busby, M.A., LL.D.	1879
Presbyterian Church in Ireland,	Rev. Matthew Leitch, D.D., D.Lit.,	1893
Wesleyan Methodists,	Rev. William Nicholas, D.D.,	1895
Association of Irish Non-Subscribing Presbyterians,	Rev. Douglas Walmsley, B.A.,	1895

APPENDIX.

Table I.

Number of Students Matriculated in Session 1898-99 :—

Matriculated in Queen's College, Belfast (Engineering), . . .	1
Admitted ad eundem, having Matriculated in the Royal University, . .	98
" " Dublin University, . .	1
	[illegible]

Table II.

A.—Numbers and Religious Persuasions of Students who have entered the College in each year since its opening.

Sessions.	Matriculated.	Non-Matriculated.	Total.	Presbyterian.	Church of Ireland.	Roman Catholic.	Methodist.	Various.	Total.
1849-50, . . .	90	105	195	145	35	3	4	8	195
1850-51, . . .	51	42	93	68	15	7	1	2	93
1851-52, . . .	49	40	89	47	25	7	9	1	89
1852-53, . . .	31	23	54	28	16	7	2	1	54
1853-54, . . .	39	23	62	36	14	5	3	4	62
1854-55, . . .	41	38	79	46	13	6	2	9	79
1855-56, . . .	33	29	62	38	17	5	2	2	63
1856-57, . . .	40	28	68	40	18	4	1	5	68
1857-58, . . .	48	23	71	53	8	6	3	–	71
1858-59, . . .	51	37	88	61	21	5	4	1	88
Entered in first 10 years,	461	393	854	562	182	60	23	26	854
1859-60, . . .	64	24	88	61	14	6	4	3	88
1860-61, . . .	96	41	137	85	29	15	3	7	137
1861-62, . . .	114	38	152	103	27	5	6	12	152
1862-63, . . .	115	22	137	92	23	19	5	5	137
1863-64, . . .	109	18	127	86	25	5	9	8	127
1864-65, . . .	109	27	136	97	23	8	8	7	135
1865-66, . . .	88	30	118	83	17	7	5	6	118
1866-67, . . .	95	12	107	61	18	6	10	14	107
1867-68, . . .	90	29	119	62	29	5	1	23	119
1868-69, . . .	79	24	103	60	15	7	8	11	103
Entered in second 10 years,	960	258	1,218	797	209	72	46	93	1,218
1869-70, . . .	[illegible]	35	98	54	23	8	1	9	[illegible]
1870-71, . . .	84	30	114	57	29	9	8	11	114
1871-72, . . .	70	25	103	50	28	6	5	14	103
1872-73, . . .	98	14	112	65	33	6	3	5	112
1873-74, . . .	98	25	123	63	28	6	13	13	123
1874-75, . . .	106	38	144	78	33	3	5	15	134
1875-76, . . .	91	24	115	69	18	10	7	11	115
1876-77, . . .	119	32	151	93	35	3	8	12	151
1877-78, . . .	118	28	146	79	31	10	9	15	146
1878-79, . . .	123	32	155	84	36	18	7	8	155
Entered in third 10 years,	995	257	1,252	[illegible]	[illegible]	64	73	113	[illegible]

A.—NUMBERS and RELIGIOUS PERSUASIONS of STUDENTS who have entered the COLLEGE in each year since its opening—*continued.*

Sessions.	Matriculated.	Non-Matriculated.	Total.	Presbyterian.	Church of Ireland.	Roman Catholic.	Methodist.	Various.	Total.
1879-80, ...	128	23	151	98	29	10	16	12	151
1880-81, ...	135	15	150	91	30	8	4	17	150
1881-82, ...	171	15	186	110	29	11	17	20	186
1882-83, ...	107	73	130	75	25	5	8	17	130
1883-84, ...	117	16	133	82	23	4	9	16	133
1884-85, ...	110	21	131	92	28	3	7	18	131
1885-86, ...	104	27	131	79	23	9	10	10	131
1886-87, ...	87	23	116	79	17	-	10	4	116
1887-88, ...	94	15	109	76	20	3	6	4	109
1888-89, ...	106	20	126	89	25	6	-	8	126
Entered in fourth 10 years,	1,159	198	1,357	853	257	58	81	118	1,357
1889-90, ...	142	28	170	104	38	6	15	15	170
1890-91, ...	110	17	127	87	23	5	6	6	127
1891-92, ...	136	20	156	103	25	7	11	18	156
1892-93, ...	88	7	97	68	11	7	4	5	97
1893-94, ...	83	29	112	63	21	10	18	5	119
1894-95, ...	93	25	117	72	21	7	7	7	117
1895-96, ...	97	13	119	74	24	8	3	5	113
1896-97, ...	87	21	108	70	15	4	6	13	108
1897-98, ...	98	17	115	69	21	7	9	6	113
1898-99, ...	88	13	101	61	18	6	4	11	101
Entered in fifth 10 years,	1,023	190	1,213	772	219	65	73	82	1,213
Total, ...	4,[illegible]	1,2[illegible]	5,[illegible]	2,985	1,133	319	380	437	5,[illegible]

B.—NUMBERS and RELIGIOUS PERSUASIONS of STUDENTS attending the COLLEGE in each Session from its opening.

Sessions.	Matriculated.	Non-Matriculated.	Total.	Presbyterian.	Church of Ireland.	Roman Catholic.	Methodist.	Various.	Total.
1849-50, ...	98	165	195	145	33	5	4	8	195
1850-51, ...	110	75	185	136	33	10	4	2	185
1851-52, ...	120	69	189	129	40	14	5	1	189
1852-53, ...	101	53	154	108	33	15	4	2	154
1853-54, ...	114	54	168	107	36	14	6	5	168
1854-55, ...	110	65	183	131	34	14	3	1	183
1855-56, ...	119	74	193	131	33	19	5	5	193
1856-57, ...	136	58	194	131	35	14	3	11	194
1857-58, ...	153	51	207	154	31	14	4	4	207
1858-59, ...	160	63	223	153	45	14	8	3	223
Average of first 10 years,	129·1	67·0	189·1	131·7	35·3	13·3	4·6	4·3	189·1
1859-60, ...	199	58	257	184	43	16	8	6	257
1860-61, ...	239	73	312	216	57	22	7	10	312
1861-62, ...	299	76	375	266	59	17	13	20	375
1862-63, ...	335	53	388	276	61	24	11	17	388
1863-64, ...	348	47	387	281	63	26	18	27	387
1864-65, ...	356	49	405	285	58	22	9	31	405
1865-66, ...	360	53	413	291	68	19	13	42	413
1866-67, ...	357	80	397	225	57	19	18	48	397
1867-68, ...	357	33	390	233	59	14	25	57	390
1868-69, ...	330	30	363	235	51	15	25	56	363
Average of second 10 years	317·2	51·0	361·2	241·6	56·8	19·4	11·6	33·2	361·2

B.—Numbers and Religious Persuasions of Students attending the College, in each Session from its opening—*con.*

Sessions.	Matriculated	Non-Matriculated	Total	Presbyterians.	Church of Ireland	Roman Catholics.	Methodists.	Various.	Total
1869-70,	328	25	353	214	57	18	19	45	353
1870-71,	337	43	380	226	76	14	22	42	380
1871-72,	305	53	358	203	80	17	13	46	358
1872-73,	328	23	351	205	79	15	21	30	351
1873-74,	344	31	375	201	87	17	29	41	375
1874-75,	346	47	393	223	85	11	24	50	393
1875-76,	353	40	393	222	70	17	29	55	393
1876-77,	393	44	437	270	85	18	29	39	437
1877-78,	421	42	463	285	80	20	27	41	463
1878-79,	453	47	500	279	80	29	33	68	500
Average of third 10 years,	362·8	37·5	400·3	236·5	76·6	16·7	24·2	43·6	400·3
1879-80,	456	38	494	331	81	22	26	34	494
1880-81,	483	26	509	326	89	22	33	48	509
1881-82,	541	26	567	355	104	25	30	55	567
1882-83,	473	29	502	305	91	20	33	53	502
1883-84,	456	25	481	280	85	17	34	55	481
1884-85,	418	31	449	280	81	19	32	46	449
1885-86,	416	44	460	282	80	17	34	47	460
1886-87,	387	36	423	281	61	9	37	35	423
1887-88,	398	31	429	290	64	13	30	32	429
1888-89,	391	31	422	305	50	11	33	27	422
Average fourth 10 years,	441·8	31·7	473·5	301·1	78·6	16·5	30·0	43·3	473·6
1889-90,	411	50	461	307	74	16	27	37	461
1890-91,	432	17	449	299	65	17	27	38	449
1891-92,	436	17	453	321	67	20	33	39	453
1892-93,	414	28	442	309	58	18	28	31	442
1893-94,	390	45	435	283	66	22	29	35	435
1894-95,	340	46	386	253	63	21	27	22	386
1895-96,	355	37	392	264	68	19	25	21	392
1896-97,	334	46	380	259	68	18	24	32	380
1897-98,	343	43	386	251	60	16	26	33	386
1898-99,	324	35	359	236	51	13	26	33	359
Average fifth 10 years,	373·9	42·8	416·7	279·5	61·2	17·1	27·2	31·1	416·7

TABLE III.

NUMBER of STUDENTS attending each Faculty in Session 1898–99.

Arts,	196
Law,	16
Medicine,	[illegible]
Engineering,	14
	362
Attending in more than one Faculty,	3
	359

TABLE IV.

NUMBER of STUDENTS who came from each of the PROVINCES of IRELAND, and from other Places.

Ulster,	326	United States,	2
Munster,	3	Belgium,	1
Leinster,	7	Spain,	1
Connaught,	8	Syria,	2
England,	7	Buenos Ayres,	1
Scotland,	5		
Canada,	1	Total,	360

TABLE V.

AGES of STUDENTS in ATTENDANCE.

Under Seventeen years,	3
From Seventeen to Eighteen,	17
From Eighteen to Nineteen,	35
From Nineteen to Twenty,	47
From Twenty to Twenty-one,	54
Above Twenty-one years,	203
Total,	359

TABLE VI.

NUMBER of LECTURES given by each Professor, and NUMBER of STUDENTS attending them, in Session 1898–99.

—	Number of Lectures.	Number of Students.
Greek,	283*	59
Latin,	272†	73
English Language and Literature,	168	56
History,	70	6
French,	200	30
German,	88	4
Logic,	108	36
Metaphysics,	77	27
Mathematics,	246	60
Natural Philosophy,	234	113
Physical Laboratory,	103	60
Chemistry,	100	59
Practical Chemistry, Summer, 1898,	54	39
Do., Winter, 1898–99,	58	26
Laboratory, Summer, 1898,	54‡	7
Do., Winter, 1898–99,	100‡	10
Zoology,	57	39
Botany, Summer, 1898,	42	61
Geology and Mineralogy,	40	8
Practical Biology, 2 hours each, Summer, 1898,	25	38
English Law,	48	16
Jurisprudence and Civil Law,	48	22
Political Economy,	74	13
Anatomy, Junior and Senior,	147	99
Practical Anatomy,	§	117
Physiology,	108	69
Practical Physiology,	18	30
Practical Histology,	24	20
Biological Chemistry,	∥	8
Medicine,	78	36
Surgery,	79	39
Operative Surgery, Summer, 1898,	37	32
Midwifery,	84	33
Materia Medica,	85	33
Ophthalmology and Otology	33	27
Sanitary Science,	37	34
Medical Jurisprudence, Summer, 1898,	27	38
Engineering,	277¶	14
Systematic Pathology, Summer, 1898,	40	39
Practical Pathology, 2 hours each, Summer, 1898,	24	33
Practical Pharmacy, Summer, 1898,	29	29
Bacteriology, Summer, 1898,	30	7

* In addition, sixty-two Lectures were given by the Senior Scholar.
† In addition, fifty-nine Lectures were given by the Senior Scholar.
‡ Days on which the Laboratory was open under the supervision of the Professors.
§ Daily during the Session from 9 to 4.
∥ Laboratory open daily during the Second Term.
¶ In addition instruction given in Office Work on 25 days.

TABLE VII.

A.—COLLEGE SCHOLARS AND PRIZEMEN.

SESSION 1898–99.

SENIOR SCHOLARS.

GREEK AND LATIN LANGUAGES, AND ANCIENT HISTORY.

Paul, Francis James, B.A.

MATHEMATICS.

Toombe, Archibald Stuart, B.A.

NATURAL PHILOSOPHY.

M'Kinstry, Archibald, B.A.

LOGIC, METAPHYSICS, AND POLITICAL ECONOMY.

M'Murray, William Bolen, B.A.	*Johnston, John James Knox*, B.A. —A prize.

NATURAL HISTORY.

Heron, Archibald George, B.A.

JUNIOR SCHOLARS.

FACULTY OF ARTS.

Third Year.

LITERARY DIVISION.

Greer, Robert Francis.	Glover, James Sands.
Clark, Andrew.	Elliott, George Reddell.
Malet, Christopher Leycester.	Pyper, James.

SCIENCE DIVISION.

Martin, James Rea.	Gillespie, Alfred Joseph.
Vinycomb, Thomas Bernard.	

Second Year.

LITERARY DIVISION.

Knox, Wm. George.	Kerr, Hugh.
Ferguson, James.	Stoupe, Margaret.
Archer, John.	M'Cullough, Reid.

SCIENCE DIVISION.

M'Donnell, John.
Park, John Edgar. } Equal.
Millar, George Crothers. }
Elliott, David Boggs.

First Year.

LITERARY DIVISION.

M'Kee, Thomas.	Wilson, William James.
Smiley, Sara Roberta Beatty.	*Houston, Robert Martin.*
Hagan, Edward James.	Leighton, Robert Henry.
Madill, James Millar Moorhead.	

SCIENCE DIVISION.

Hawthorne, William.	Browne, David John.
Houston, Robert Martin.	*Hagan, Edward James.*
Houston, Charles Cornelius.	Thompson, John Knox.

Faculty of Medicine.

Fifth Year.

Medicine and Pathology.	*Surgery and Midwifery.*
Hunter, William Matthew.	Clements, John Edmund.

Fourth Year.

Baldcliffe, John Alexander Douglas.	Rankin, John C.
	M'Ilwaine, John Elder.—A Prize.

Third Year.

Black, Albert Lytle.	M'Mordie, David.

Second Year.

Johnston, Henry Mulrea.	*M'Clatchey, John.*—A Prize.
Carswaith, Thomas.	

First Year.

Literary Division.—Pyper, John Stanley.

Faculty of Law.

Second Year.

Hanna, John, B.A.	Clements, Mary Elizabeth, B.A.

First Year.

Nevin, William Munson, LL.B.	Macartney, Robert James, B.A.

School of Engineering.

Third Year.
Shaw, John White.

Second Year.
Agnew, Alexander.

First Year.
Alexander, Conoel William Long.

Private Endowments.

Dunville Students.

Megaw, John Wallace Dick, B.A., elected 1897.
Rice, James, B.A., „ 1898.

Andrews Student.

Caldwell, William, B.A., elected 1897.

Porter Scholars.

Smyth, Samuel Andrew, elected 1897.
Greer, Robert Francis, „ 1898.

Sullivan Scholars.

M'Clatchey, John, elected 1896.	Hagan, Edward James, elected 1898.
Miller, George Crockett, „ 1897	

Sir Hercules Pakenham Scholar.

Rutherford, John Finlay, elected 1897.

Emily Lady Pakenham Scholar.

M'Kee, Phineas, elected 1898.

Blayney Exhibitioner.

Paul, Francis James, B.A.

Class Prizemen.

Arts.

Greek.

Honour Class.

Greer, Robert Francis. | Clark, Andrew.
Elliott, George Reddell.

Second Year.

Knox, William George. | Kerr, Hugh.

First Year.

M'Kee, Phineas.
Madill, James Millar Moorhead, } equal.
Smiley, Sara Robena Beatty.

Latin.

Honour Class.

Clark, Andrew. | Elliott, George Reddell.
Greer, Robert Francis.

Second Year.

Kerr, Hugh. | Knox, William George.

First Year.

Wilson, William James. | M'Kee, Phineas.
Smiley, Sara Robena Beatty. | Hagan, Edward James.

English Language and Literature.

Third Year.

Greer, Robert Francis, } equal.
Macartney, Robert James, B.A.,

Second Year.

Kerr, Hugh. | Rutherford, John Finlay.
Park, John Edgar.

First Year.

Wilson, William James. | Hawthorne, William.
Hotson, Robert Martin. | M'Kee, Phineas.

French.

Third Year.

Molat, Christopher Leycester.

Second Year.

Elliott, David Boggs, } equal.
Knox, William George,

First Year.

M'Kee, Phineas.
Madill, James Millar Moorhead, } equal.
Wilson, William James,

German.

Second Year.

Rutherford, John Finlay.

First Year.

Hawthorne, William.

MATHEMATICS.

Honour Class.

Stewart, Samuel Edgar. | Martin, James Rea.

Second Year.

M'Donnell, John. | Agnew, Alexander.
Millar, George Crockett.

First Year.

Hawthorne, William. | Houston, Robert Martin.

MATHEMATICAL PHYSICS.

Honour Class.

Martin, James Rea.

Second Year.

M'Donnell, John.

EXPERIMENTAL PHYSICS.

Honour Class.

Vinycomb, Thomas Bernard.

First Year

(Arts, Engineering, and Medicine).

Hawthorne, William. | Lloyd, Reginald Thornton.
Lyle, Thomas. | M'Pherson, Joseph Clarke.
Alexander, Connel William Long, } equal
Coates, Foster, }

LOGIC.

Honour Class.

M'Whirter, James.

Second Year.

Park, John Edgar, } equal. | Elliott, David Beggs, } equal
Taylor, John Moreton, } | Kerr, Hugh, }

METAPHYSICS.

M'Whirter, James. | Greer, Robert Francis.

POLITICAL ECONOMY.

Murray, Robert Henry, B.A. | Greer, Robert Francis.

JURISPRUDENCE.

Greer, Robert Francis. | Clark, Andrew.

ENGINEERING.

Second Year.

Owens, Robert Black.

First Year.

Heron, James.

GEOLOGY.

Shaw, John White.

MEDICINE.

ZOOLOGY.

Senior Division.

Moore, James Herbert.

Junior Division.

M'Pherson, Joseph Clarke.
Milligan, Ernest Marcus Henry.

Lyle, Thomas.
Carlisle, David John,
Moffett, George Baird, } equal.

CHEMISTRY.

Senior.

Lloyd, Reginald Thornton (Engineering).

Junior.

Milligan, Ernest Marcus Henry.

Lyle, Thomas.

PRACTICAL CHEMISTRY.

Senior.

Bethune, Robert James.

M'Clatchey, John.

Junior.

Dick, Alexander,
Forbes, Hugh John,
Liddle, Thomas Dixon, } equal.

CHEMICAL LABORATORY.

Vinycomb, Thomas Bernard (Arts).

SYSTEMATIC ANATOMY.

Senior.

M'Mordie, David, B.A.

Junior.

Johnston, Henry Malres.
Bright, William Henry Norman.

M'Clatchey, John.

PRACTICAL ANATOMY.

Third Year.

Gill, John Henry,
M'Mordie, David, B.A. } equal.

M'Crea, Hugh Moreland.

Second Year.

Phillips, Walter,
Stewart, Robert Alex., } equal.

Blakely, Sydney Herbert George.

First Year.

Babington, James Wm. Herbert.
Killen, Thomas.

Bright, William Henry Norman.

Physiology and Histology.

Senior.

M'Mordie, David, B.A.	Black, Albert Lytle.
Hunter, Samuel Robert.	

Junior.

Johnston, Henry Mulree.

Practical Histology.

Campbell, James Graham.	Wilson, James Edwin.
Weir, John Stewart Ferguson.	

Medicine.

Hogg, William John.	Milliken, David.

Surgery.

Gray, Thomas.	Mathewson, Robert.
Logan, Thomas Stratford.	

Materia Medica.

M'Clure, Samuel.	Fergus, William John Brereton.

Midwifery, Gynæcology, and Diseases of Children.

Andrews, Marion Braidfoot, } equal.	*Geffikin, Prudence Elizabeth, non-matriculated.*
Steen, Hugh Barkley, } equal.	Stewart, Joseph.
Gray Thomas.	

Ophthalmology and Otology.

Rankin, John Campbell.	Clements, John Edmund.
MacIlwaine, John Elder.	

Law.

Equity and Common Law.

Hanna, John, B.A.	Clements, Mary Elizabeth, M.A.
Beaumont, John Montgomery, non-matriculated.	

Civil Law.

Clements, Mary Elizabeth, M.A., } equal
Hanna, John, } equal

First Year.

Law of Property.

Nevin, William Manson, LL.B.	Macartney, Robert James, M.A.

Jurisprudence.

Nevin, William Manson, LL.B.	Macartney, Robert James, M.A.

Summer Prizemen, 1898.

Botany.

Blakely, Sydney Herbert George.
Bethune, Robert James.
Johnston, Henry Mulrea.
M'Clatchey, John.
Campbell, James Hamilton.
Small, James Kennedy.

Practical Chemistry.

Senior.

Rodgers, William, M.A.

Junior.

Knox, John.
Whyte, Samuel Hugh.
M'Cloy, Alexander.

Systematic Pathology.

Hunter, William Matthew.
Steen, Robert.
Crawford, Annie Helen.

Practical Pharmacy.

Rolord, John Hope, B.A.
Andrews, Marion Braidfoot.

B.—Degrees, Diplomas, Honours, &c., obtained by Students of the College at the Examinations of the Royal University of Ireland in 1898.

Junior Fellowship.

In Mathematics.

Houston, William A., M.A.

University Studentship.

In Ancient Classics.

Henry, Robert M.

University Medical Studentship.

Houston, Thomas, B.A., M.B., B.CH., B.A.O.

SCHOLARSHIP IN ANCIENT CLASSICS.

Second Class.

Stoupe, Margaret.

IN MATHEMATICS

First Class.

M'Donnell, John.

FACULTY OF ARTS.

M.A. DEGREE EXAMINATION.

Autumn, 1898.

Honours.

ANCIENT CLASSICS.

First Class.

Henry, Robert M.

Honours.

MENTAL AND MORAL SCIENCE.

Second Class.

Tuel, William H. C. W.

HISTORY AND POLITICAL SCIENCE.

Pass.

Allen, David.

B.A. DEGREE EXAMINATION.

Summer, 1898.

Pass.

Kenny, Francis.
Kyle, John.
MacGiffin, Henry A.
Wilson, Norman.

Autumn, 1898.

EXHIBITIONS.

The following Candidates were qualified upon their answering to obtain Exhibitions; the names of those disqualified by age or otherwise are printed in *italics*. The names in each Class are arranged in alphabetical order.

First Class—£18 each.

Hawthorne, John.

Second Class—£21 each.

M'Cutcheon, Katherine S. H.
M'Kinstry, Archibald.
Peden, Thomas U. (Sch.)
Tombe, Archibald S. (Sch.)

HONOURS IN ANCIENT CLASSICS.

Second Class.

Wilson, George (Sch.)

HONOURS IN MENTAL AND MORAL SCIENCE

Second Class.

M'Murray, William B.

LOGIC, METAPHYSICS, HISTORY OF PHILOSOPHY, AND POLITICAL ECONOMY.

Pass.

Johnston, John J. K.

HONOURS IN CIVIL AND CONSTITUTIONAL HISTORY, POLITICAL ECONOMY, AND GENERAL JURISPRUDENCE.

Second Class.

Dennan, William.

Pass.

Davidson, William M.
Jordan, Sarah.
Parker, Victoria.

HONOURS IN MATHEMATICAL SCIENCE.

First Class.

Tombe, Archibald S. (Sch.)

HONOURS IN MATHEMATICAL AND EXPERIMENTAL PHYSICS.

Second Class.

M'Kinstry, Archibald.

HONOURS IN EXPERIMENTAL SCIENCE.

First Class.

Hawthorne, John.

Pass.

Jones, George J.

CHEMISTRY AND PHYSIOLOGY.

Pass.

Caughey, Robert H.
Phillips, Walter.

Second University Examination in Arts.

Summer, 1898.

Exhibitions.

First Class, £30 each.

Greer, Robert F. (Sch.)
Glover, James S.
Martin, James R. (Sch.).

Second Class, £18 each.

Elliott, George R. (Sch.)
Clark, Andrew.
Vinycomb, Thomas B.
Waddell, John (Sch.)

Honours in Latin.

First Class.

Greer, Robert F. (Sch.).
Clark, Andrew.
Elliott, George R. (Sch.)

Second Class.

Waddell, John (Sch.)
Malet, Christopher L.

Honours in Greek.

First Class.

Elliott, George R. (Sch.)
Greer, Robert F. (Sch.)

Second Class.

Clark, Andrew.

Honours in English.

Second Class.

Greer, Robert F. (Sch.)
Clark, Andrew.
Rea, Thomas.
Elliott, George R. (Sch.)

Honours in Mathematics.

Second Class.

Martin, James R. (Sch.)
Vinycomb, Thomas B.

Honours in French.

First Class.

Rea, Thomas.

Honours in German.

Second Class.

Rea, Thomas.

Honours in Mathematical Physics.

First Class.

Vinycomb, Thomas B.	Martin, James B. (Sch.)

Honours in Experimental Physics.

First Class.

Martin, James B. (Sch.)	Vinycomb, Thomas B.

Honours in Chemistry.

Second Class.

Vinycomb, Thomas B.

Pass List.

Armour, William.
Buchanan, John D.
Carnwath, Thomas.
Clark, Andrew.
Davis, William H.
Elliott, George R. (Sch.)
Gillespie, Alfred J.
Glover, James S.
Greer, Robert F. (Sch.)
Hanna, Samuel.
Henry, James T.
Irwin, Samuel J.
Killen, Thomas.
Lynd, Robert W.
M'Clatchey, John.
M'Clure, William.
M'Connell, James.
Magill, John F. G.
Malet, Christopher L.
Martin, James B. (Sch.)
Millar, Robert.
Milligan, Ernest H. M.
Owens, Robert B.
Pyper, James.
Rea, Thomas.
Rutherford, Andrew A.
Simms, Alexander.
Thomson, Lawrence W.
Vinycomb, Thomas B.
Waddell, John (Sch.)
Wilson, James E.
Woods, Robert S.

First University Examination in Arts.

Summer, 1898.

Exhibitions.

First Class, £30 each.

Adamson, Francis L. (Sch.)	Kerr, Hugh.

Second Class, £15 each.

Stouppe, Margaret.
M'Donnell, John.
Ferguson, James.
Knox, William G.
Rutherford, John F.
M'Cullough, Reid.

HONOURS IN LATIN.

First Class.

Adamson, Francis L. (Sch.)

Second Class.

Ferguson, James.
Stouppe, Margaret.
Kerr, Hugh.
Knox, William G.
Rutherford, John F.
Archer, John.

HONOURS IN GREEK.

First Class.

Adamson, Francis L. (Sch.)
Stouppe, Margaret

Second Class.

Knox, William G.

HONOURS IN ENGLISH.

First Class.

Kerr, Hugh.
Adamson, Francis L. (Sch.)
Stouppe, Margaret,

Second Class.

M'Cullough, Reid.

HONOURS IN MATHEMATICS.

First Class.

M'Donnell, John.

Second Class.

Miller, George C.
Park, John E.

HONOURS IN NATURAL PHILOSOPHY.

Second Class.

Adamson, Francis L. (Sch.)

The following Candidates were also declared qualified to compete for Honours, but some of them did not present themselves for the Oral Examination :—

GREEK.

Ferguson, James.

ENGLISH.

Park, John E.
Rutherford, John F.

MATHEMATICS.

Kerr. Hugh.

Pass.

Adams, Samuel K.	M'Donnell, John.
Adamson, Francis L. (Sch.)	Magill, Joseph A.
Agnew, Alexander.	Millar, George C.
Archer, John.	Morton, John G.
Cowdy, John.	Park, John E.
Ferguson, James.	Parker, Samuel J.
Kerr, Hugh.	Patterson, Thomas.
Knox, William G.	Pyper, John S.
Legate, John N. M.	Rowan, William J.
Lloyd, Reginald T.	Rutherford, John F.
Lyle, Thomas.	Stoupps, Margaret.
M'Cullough, Reid.	

First University Examination in Arts.

Autumn, 1898.

Pass.

Coulter, Thomas J.	Simpson, David B.
Lowry, Charles G.	Stephens, John K.
Mayberry, William J.	

Faculty of Law.

LL.B. Degree Examination.

Summer, 1898.

Exhibition.

First Class, £42.

M'Cutcheon, Robert B.

Honours.

First Class.

M'Cutcheon, Robert B.

Pass.

Dickson, Robert J.	Whitaker, Herbert T.

First Examination in Law.

Summer, 1898.

Pass.

Hanna, John.

Faculty of Medicine.

M.D. Degree Examination.

Spring, 1898.

M'Burney, John H., M.B.

Autumn, 1898.

Davidson, Isaac A., B.A., M.B., B.CH., B.A.O.

MEDICAL DEGREES EXAMINATION (M.B., B.CH., B.A.O.)

Spring, 1898.

Upper Pass.

Brown, David.

Pass.

Armstrong, William L.
Greenfield, Thomas K.
Hogg, George A.
Mawhirter, William H. W.
Wilson, William J.

MEDICAL DEGREES EXAMINATION (M.B. B.CH. B.A.O.).

Autumn, 1898.

EXHIBITIONS.

Second Class, £25.

M'Cay, David.

HONOURS.

Second Class.

M'Cay, David,

Upper Pass Division.

Harbinson, George C. B.
M'Master, Arthur H.
Martin, Joseph.

Pass.

Graham, Robert A. L., B.A.
Graham, Alexander
Knight, Alexander E.
Neilson, Robert A.
Orr, Henry S.
Robinson, Daniel S.
Shannon, William J., B.A.
Shaw, Robert A.
Whyte, James E.

THIRD EXAMINATION IN MEDICINE.

Spring, 1898

Upper Pass.

Byers, Isaac M.

Pass.

Barbour, John H.
Gillespie, John R., M.A.
Hinton, Alexandrina C.
Kennedy, Alexander F.
Kennedy, Thomas.
M'Carrison, Robert.
Martin, Edwin W. S.
Rowan, Marriott L., B.A.
Spence, William A. C.
Waddell, James.

THIRD EXAMINATION IN MEDICINE.

Autumn, 1898.

EXHIBITIONS.

Second Class, £30.

MacIlwaine, John E.

Second Class, £20.

Radcliffe, John A. D.

HONOURS.

First Class.

MacIlwaine, John E.

Second Class.

Radcliffe, John A. D.

Upper Pass.

Rankin, John C.

Pass Division.

Brown, John W., B.A.
Crooks, Emily M.
Donnelly, Hugh.
Gibson, John M'C.
Gray, Thomas.
Mathewson, Robert.
Reford, John H., B.A.
Robb, James J.
Rutherford, Henry E.
Steen, Hugh B.
Stevenson, Howard, B.A.
Stewart, Joseph.
Tierney, John.

SECOND EXAMINATION IN MEDICINE.

Spring, 1898.

EXHIBITIONS.

Second Class, £15.

M'Mordie, David, B.A.

HONOURS.

Second Class.

M'Mordie, David, B.A.

Upper Pass.

Heron, Archibald G., B.A.
Thomson, Alfred M.

Pass.

Kennedy, Robert.
M'Crea, John, B.A.
Smith, Hugh B.
Thompson, William J.
Watson, William.

SECOND EXAMINATION IN MEDICINE.

Autumn, 1898.

EXHIBITION.

Second Class, £15.

Black, Albert L.

HONOURS.

Second Class.

Black, Albert L.

Upper Pass.

Armstrong, John.
Hunter, Samuel B.
M'Cloy, Alexander.
M'Clure, Samuel.
M'Crea, Hugh M.

Pass.

Agnew, Henry M.
Campbell, David R.
Ferguson, William J. B.
Ferris, John H.
Fisher, Robert W.
Gill, John H.
Gillespie, James.
Knox, John.
Lake, George F.
M'Candless, Richard.
M'Caughey, Francis H.
M'Cone, Francis E.
M'Murray, John.
Mann, Frederick C.
Martin, James F. G.
Rodgers, William, M.A.
Stewart, Robert A.

FIRST EXAMINATION IN MEDICINE.
Summer, 1898.

EXHIBITIONS.

The following Candidates were qualified upon their answering to obtain Exhibitions; the names of those disqualified by standing or otherwise are printed in italics:—

Second Class, £10.

M'Clatchey, John. | Johnston, Henry M.

HONOURS IN BOTANY.
Second Class.
Johnston, Henry M.

HONOURS IN CHEMISTRY.
First Class.
M'Clatchey, John.

HONOURS IN EXPERIMENTAL PHYSICS.
Second Class.
M'Clatchey, John. | Irwin, Samuel T.

Pass.

Belknap, Robert J.
Blakely, Sydney H. G.
Buchanan, John D.
Campbell, James H.
Carswaith, Thomas.
Cummings, William.
Dale, John W.
Harper, Rodolphus W.
Hayden, William R.
Irwin, Samuel T.
Johnston, Henry M.
Killen, James W.
Killen, Thomas.
M'Clatchey, John.
Moore, Samuel E. W.
Small, James K.
Smyth, Frederick C.
Stockman, Samuel.
Thompson, Joseph H.
Wilson, James E.

FIRST EXAMINATION IN MEDICINE.
Autumn, 1898.
Pass.

Davis, William H.
Dick, Alexander.
Killen, Samuel J.
Suffern, Charles E.
Suffern, Thomas H.
Toner, Margaret.
Wilson, James W. A.

SCHOOL OF ENGINEERING.
Summer, 1898.
B. E. DEGREE EXAMINATION.
Pass.

Duffield, Hugh J. | MacGiffin, Henry A.

SECOND PROFESSIONAL EXAMINATION IN ENGINEERING.
Summer, 1898.
HONOURS.
Second Class.
Shaw, John W.

Pass.

M'Turk, Alexander. | Watson, John F.

FIRST PROFESSIONAL EXAMINATION IN ENGINEERING.
Pass.

Agnew, Alexander.
Munce, James S.
Owens, Robert B.

TABLE VIII.—STUDENTS OF THE COLLEGE WHO HAVE GAINED JUNIOR FELLOWSHIPS, STUDENTSHIPS, SCHOLARSHIPS, EXHIBITIONS, OR PRIZES IN THE ROYAL UNIVERSITY OF IRELAND, SINCE ITS ESTABLISHMENT.

The names of those who were disqualified by University standing, or age, are printed in *Italics*.

JUNIOR FELLOWSHIPS.

Morton, William B., M.A., in Mathematics, 1894.
Woodburn, George, M.A., in Mental and Moral Science, 1894.
M'Elderry, Robert K., M.A., in Classics, 1896.
Donnan, Frederick G., M.A., in Chemistry, with Experimental Physics, 1897.
Houston, William A., M.A., in Mathematics, 1898.

UNIVERSITY STUDENTSHIPS.

Tate, James, in Mathematics, 1883, £100 for five years.
M'Quitty, William B., in Experimental Science, 1884, £100 for five years.
FitzHenry, William A., in Mental and Moral Science, 1885, £100 for five years.
Boyd, Andrew, in Civil and Constitutional History, Jurisprudence, and Political Philosophy, 1886, £100 for five years.
Orr, William McFadden, in Mathematics, 1887, £100 for five years.
Bowan, William H., in Classics, 1889, £100 for three years.
Woodburn, George, in Mental and Moral Science, 1889, £100 for three years.
Montgomery, Robert, in Classics, 1891, £100 for three years.
Haslett, Thomas, in Mental and Moral Science, 1891, £100 for three years.
Morton, William B., in Mathematical Science, 1892, £100 for three years.
Moore, Benjamin, in Experimental Science, 1893, £100 for three years.
M'Elderry, Robert K., in Classics, 1893, £100 for three years.
Cochrane, John, in History and Political Science, 1893, £100 for three years.
Donnan, Frederick G., in Experimental Science, 1894, £100 for three years.
Leathem, John G., in Mathematical Science, 1895, £100 for three years.
Magill, Robert, in Mental and Moral Science, 1896, £100 for three years.
Houston, William A., in Mathematical Science, 1896, £100 for three years.
Gillespie, John R., in Experimental Science, 1896, £100 for three years.
Henry, Robert M., in Classics, 1893, £100 for three years.

UNIVERSITY MEDICAL STUDENTSHIP.

Johnstone, Robert J., 1896, £200 for two years.
Houston, Thomas, 1898, £200 for two years.

UNIVERSITY SCHOLARSHIPS.

Orr, William M'F., in Mathematics, 1883, £50 for three years.
Johnson, William S., in Classics, 1884, £50 for three years.
Alexander, John J., in Mathematics, 1884, £50 for three years.
Everett, Alice, in Mathematics, 1885, £50 for three years.
Porter, William H., in Classics, 1885, £50 for three years.
Haslett, William W., in Classics, 1886, £50 for three years.
Williamson, William H., in Mathematics, 1886, £50 for three years.
Major, Harold W., in Mathematics, 1888, £50 for three years.
Stoupe, Margaret, Second Class in Classics, 1898, £20 for three years.
M'Donnell, John, First Class in Mathematics, £40 for three years.

Dr. Henry Hutchinson Stewart Scholarships.

Wilson, Mary, in Arts, 1888.
Baxter, James S., in Arts, 1890.
Woods, William J., in Medicine, 1890.
Chapman, Agnes H., in Arts, 1892.

At M.A. Examination.

Louden, James, a Gold Medal, 1881.
Boyd, Andrew, a Special Prize, 1885, £20.
FitzHenry, William A., a Gold Medal, 1886.
M'Quitty, William B., a Special Prize, 1885, £20.
Hunter, James, a Special Prize, 1886, £50.
Orr, William McF., a Gold Medal, 1887.
Campbell, John E., a Special Prize, 1887, £50.
Woodburn, George, a Gold Medal, 1889.
Witherow, James M., a Special Prize, 1891, £50.
Haslett, William W., Special Prize, 1892, £50.
Heron, Richard C., Special Prize, 1893, £40.

At B.A. Examination.

Harrison, Thomas,	First Class	Exhibition,	1882,	—
Johnston, John,	„	„	„	£50.
Jones, Robert M.,	„	„	„	£50.
M'Vicker, John W.,	„	„	„	£50.
Campbell, John E.,	„	„	1883	£50.
Darbishire, Herbert D.,	„	„	„	£50.
Hunter, James,	„	„	„	£50.
Louden, James,	„	„	„	£30.
Campbell, John,	Second Class	„	„	£25.
Chambers, Joseph,	„	„	„	—
Boyd, Andrew,	First Class	„	1884,	£50.
Boyd, Robert W.,	„	„	„	—
FitzHenry, William A.,	„	„	„	£50
M'Quitty, William B.,	„	„	„	£50.
Glass, Thomas,	Second Class	„	„	—
Henderson, Robert,	„	„	„	£25.
Killen, William M.,	„	„	„	£25.
M'Aulis, Thomas,	„	„	„	£25.
Russell, William A.,	„	„	„	£25.
Cummins, David,	First Class	„	1885,	—
Orr, William M'F.,	„	„	„	£50.
Orr, William M'F.,	Special Prize,		„	£50
Rea, James C.,	First Class	Exhibition,	„	—
Russell, William,	„	„	„	£50.
Stewart, Thomas,	„	„	„	£50.
Vance, John,	„	„	„	£50.
Crossle, Edward S.,	Second Class	„	„	£25.
Dill, Alexander H.,	„	„	„	—
Donald, Robert J. F.,	„	„	„	—
Fitzsimmons, James H.,	„	„	„	£25.
M'Neill, Robert,	„	„	„	£25
Priestley, James,	„	„	„	£25.
Alexander, John J.,	First Class	„	1886,	£50.
Dunn, William,	„	„	„	£50.
Johnson, William S.,	„	„	„	£50.
Wheeler, George H.,	„	„	„	£50.

AT B.A. EXAMINATION—*con.*

Jamison, Daniel,	Second Class	Exhibition,	1886,	£25.
Montgomery, Robert,	"	"	"	—
Rowan, William H.,	First Class	"	1887,	£50.
Brown, Richard R.,	Second Class	"	"	—
Browne, James A.,	"	"	"	£25.
Campbell, Robert,	"	"	"	£25.
Henderson, William,	"	"	"	£25.
Knightley, Frederick R.,	"	"	"	—
McConnell, James,	"	"	"	—
Salters, James,	"	"	"	—
Wilson, Mary,	"	"	"	£25.
Allison, William M. R.,	First Class	"	1888,	£50.
Haslett, William W.,	"	"	"	£50.
Stewart, James A.,	"	"	"	£50.
Woodburn, George,	"	"	"	£50.
Adams, John J.,	Second Class	"	"	£25.
Jackson, Maud S.,	"	"	"	—
Montgomery, Robert,	"	"	"	£25.
Semple, John,	"	"	"	—
Williamson, William H.,	"	"	"	£25
Archer, James H.,	First Class	"	1889,	£42.
Entricon, Sara,	"	"	"	—
Haslett, Thomas,	"	"	"	£42.
Kirk, Thomas S.,	"	"	"	£42.
Morton, William B.,	"	"	"	£42.
Witherow, James M.,	"	"	"	£42.
Wood, Jackson,	"	"	"	—
Cotter, William E. P.,	Second Class	"	"	£21.
Leathem, Robert R. L.,	"	"	"	£21.
Hanna, William,	First Class	"	1890,	£42.
Heron, Richard C.,	"	"	"	£42.
Cochrane, John,	Second Class	"	"	£21.
Lee, James,	"	"	"	£21.
McKee, Robert D.,	"	"	"	—
Moore, Benjamin,	"	"	"	£21.
Walker, James,	"	"	"	£21.
Wylie, John,	"	"	"	—
Leathem, John G.,	First Class	"	1891,	£42.
M'Elderry, Robert K.,	"	"	"	£42.
Baxter, James S.,	Second Class	"	"	£21.
Bradshaw, James M.,	"	"	"	£21.
Heron, James, R., B.E.,	"	"	"	—
Ashmore, Richard H.,	First Class	"	1892,	£42.
Donnan, Frederick G.,	"	"	"	£42.
Houston, William A.,	"	"	"	£42.
Gillespie, James T.,	Second Class	"	"	£21.
Morell, David E.,	"	"	"	£21.
O'Neill, Frederick W. S.,	"	"	"	£21.
Chapman, Agnes S.,	First Class	"	1893,	£42.
Gillespie, John R.,	"	"	"	£42.
Hanna, Henry,	"	"	"	£42.
Henry, Robert M.,	"	"	"	£42.
Rodgers, William,	"	"	"	£42.
Johnstone, Robt. J.,	Second Class	"	"	£21.
Martin, Thomas,	"	"	"	£21.
Sayers, Wilhelmina J.,	"	"	"	£21.
Locke, George T.,	First Class,	"	1894,	£42.
M'Mullan, John J.,	"	"	"	£42.
Magill, Robert,	"	"	"	£42.
Buchanan, James L.,	Second Class	"	"	£21.
Mickelly, William,	"	"	"	£21.
M'Cullo, James,	First Class,	"	1895,	£42

At B.A. Examination—con.

Name	Class		Year	Amount
Wallace, John S.,	First Class	Exhibition,	1895,	£42.
Brown, John W.,	Second Class	"	"	£21.
Buchanan, Alexander C.,	"	"	"	£21.
Haire, James,	"	"	"	£21
M'Bride, James A.	"	"	"	—
Magaw, John W. D.	"	"	"	£21.
Purvis, William J.	"	"	"	£21.
Rice, James,	First Class	"	1896,	£42.
Beare, Thomas J.,	Second Class	"	"	£21.
Donald, Albert L.,	"	"	"	—
Graham, Robert A. L.,	"	"	"	£21.
Hamill, William D.	"	"	"	£21.
Leathem, William H.,	"	"	"	£21.
Dunn, Andrew,	First Class	"	1897,	—
Seymour, Henry J.,	"	"	"	—
Stoops, William,	"	"	"	—
Armstrong, Fred. W.,	Second Class	"	"	£21.
Caldwell, William	"	"	"	—
Harvey, Thomas E.,	"	"	"	£21.
M'Mordie, David,	"	"	"	£21.
Paul, Francis J.,	"	"	"	£21.
Porter, Samuel C.,	"	"	"	£21.
Tord, William H. C. W.,	"	"	"	£21.
Hawthorne, John,	First Class,	"	1898,	£42.
M'Cutcheon, Catherine S. H.,	Second Class	"	"	£21.
M'Kinstry, Archibald,	"	"	"	£21.
Peden, Thomas M.,	"	"	"	£21.
Toombs, Archibald S.,	"	"	"	£21.

At Second Arts Examination.

Name	Class		Year	Amount
Russell, William A.,	First Class	Exhibition,	1882,	£40.
Darbishire, Herbert D.,	Second Class	"	"	£20.
Hunter, James,	"	"	"	£20.
Campbell, John E.,	"	"	"	£20.
Lennox, Malcolm E. M.,	First Class	"	1883,	£40.
Donald, Robert J. F.,	Second Class	"	"	£20.
Rea, James C.,	"	"	"	—
Orr, William M'F.,	First Class	"	1884,	£40.
M'Neill, Robert,	"	"	"	£40.
Cromie, Edward S.,	Second Class	"	"	£20.
Anderson, Alice M.,	"	"	"	£20.
Haslett, Annie W.,	"	"	"	£20.
Priestley, James,	"	"	"	£20.
Johnson, William S.,	First Class	"	1885,	£40.
Wheeler, George H.,	Second Class	"	"	£20.
Brown, George W.,	"	"	"	£20.
Macdonnell, Adam T. P.,	"	"	"	£20.
Irwin, William,	First Class	"	"	£20.
Dick, John S.,	"	"	"	£21.
Rowan, William H.,	"	"	1886,	£40.
Lake, Edward H.,	"	"	"	£40.
Montgomery, Robert,	"	"	"	£40.
Simm, David M.,	"	"	"	£40.
Semple, John,	Second Class	"	"	—
Campbell, Robert,	"	"	"	£20.
Everett, Alice,	"	"	"	£20
Pedlow, Thomas B.,	"	"	"	£20.

At Second Arts Examination—*con.*

Name	Class		Year	Amount
Wylie, John,	Second Class Exhibition,		1886,	£20.
Jamison, Alexander,	"	"	"	£20.
Haslett, William W.,	First Class	"	1887,	£40.
Stewart, James A.,	"	"	"	£40.
Cotter, William H. P.,	Second Class	"	"	£20.
Williamson, William H.,	"	"	"	£20.
Hamill, James,	"	"	"	£20.
Morton, William R.,	First Class	"	1888,	£40.
Archer, James H.,	"	"	"	£40.
Lee, James,	"	"	"	£40.
Megaw, Robert D.,	Second Class	"	"	£20.
Dickie, Alexander A.,	"	"	"	£20.
Fairicus, Sero,	"	"	"	...
Bradshaw, James M.,	First Class	"	1889,	£36.
Moore, Benjamin,	Second Class	"	"	£18.
Walker, James,	"	"	"	£18.
M'Cracken, William J.,	"	"	"	£18.
Heron, Richard C.,	"	"	"	£18.
Donald, Albert L.,	"	"	"	£18.
Houston, Thomas,	"	"	"	£18.
Leathem, John G.,	First Class	"	1890,	£36.
Gillespie, James T.,	"	"	"	£36.
M'Elderry, Robert K.,	"	"	"	£36.
Hunter, James S.,	"	"	"	£36.
Toye, Thomas,	Second Class	"	"	£18.
Gillespie, Samuel,	"	"	"	£18.
Megaw, David,	"	"	"	£18.
Fullerton, William A.,	"	"	"	£18.
Wilson, William A.,	"	"	"	£18.
Dornan, Frederick G.,	First Class	"	1891,	£36.
Ashmore, Richard H.,	"	"	"	£36.
Houston, William A.,	"	"	"	£36.
M'Kitrick, Alex.,	Second Class	"	"	£18.
Porter, John A.,	"	"	"	£18.
Howes, Marriott L.,	"	"	"	£18.
Gillespie, John R.,	First Class	"	1892,	£36.
Rodgers, William,	"	"	"	£36.
Crawford, William M.,	"	"	"	£36.
M'Cutcheon, Robt. R.,	Second Class	"	"	£18.
Reid, David D.,	"	"	"	£18.
Pyper, John,	"	"	"	£18.
Henry, Robert M.,	"	"	"	£18.
Locke, George T.,	First Class	"	1893,	£36.
Ross, Walter P.,	"	"	"	£36.
Blakelly, William,	"	"	"	£36.
Buchanan, James L.,	Second Class	"	"	£18.
Minford, John Y.,	"	"	"	£18.
M'Calla, James,	First Class	"	1894,	£36.
Blakelly, Samuel B.,	"	"	"	£36.
Buchanan, Alexander C.,	"	"	"	£36.
Purvis, William J.,	Second Class	"	"	£18.
Rice, James,	First Class	"	1895,	£36.
Leathem, William H.,	"	"	"	£36.
Heare, Thomas J.,	Second Class	"	"	£18.
M'Neill, William,	"	"	"	£18.
Fullerton, Joseph A.	"	"	"	£18.
Paul, Francis J.,	First Class	"	1896,	£36.
Armstrong, Fredk. W.,	Second Class	"	"	£18.
Porter, Samuel C.,	"	"	"	£18.
Harvey, Thomas E.,	"	"	"	£18.
M'Cutcheon, Katherine S. H.,	"	"	"	£18.

At Second Arts Examination—*con.*

Wilson, George,	First Class	Exhibition,	1887	£36.
Smyth, Samuel W.,	Second Class	"	"	£18.
Tombe, Archibald,	"	"	"	£18.
Stewart, Samuel F.,	"	"	"	£18.
Sinclair, William T.,	"	"	"	£18.
Greer, Robert T.,	First Class	"	1888,	£36.
Glover, James S.,	"	"	"	£36.
Martin, James R.,	"	"	"	£36.
Elliott, George H.,	Second Class	"	"	£18.
Clark, Andrew,	"	"	"	£18.
Vinycomb, Thomas B.,	"	"	"	£18.
Waddell, John,	"	"	"	£18.

At First University Examination.

Gorman, Wm. T.,	Second Class	Exhibition,	1882,	£15.
Keane, Albert T.,	"	"	"	£15.
M'Neill, Robert,	First Class	"	1883,	£30.
Orr, William M'F.,	"	"	"	£30.
Cromie, Edward S.,	Second Class	"	"	£15.
Anderson, Alice M.,	"	"	"	£15.
Brown, George W.,	First Class	"	1884,	£30.
Wheeler, George H.,	Second Class	"	"	£15.
Morton, Hamilton,	"	"	"	£15.
Alexander, John J.,	"	"	"	£15.
Irwin, William,	"	"	"	£15.
Dick, John S.,	"	"	"	£15.
Semple, John,	First Class	"	1885,	—
Everett, Alice,	"	"	"	£30.
Montgomery, Robert,	"	"	"	£30.
Rowan, William H.,	"	"	"	£30.
Lake, Edward H.,	"	"	"	£30.
Campbell, Robert,	Second Class	"	"	£15.
Pedlow, Thomas B.,	"	"	"	£15.
Hamill, James,	"	"	"	£15
Jamison, Alexander,	"	"	"	£15.
Haslett, Wm. W.,	First Class	"	1886,	£30.
Williamson, Wm. H.,	"	"	"	£30.
Cotter, Wm. E. P.,	Second Class	"	"	£15
Allison, Wm. M. B.,	"	"	"	£15
Stewart, James A.,	"	"	"	£15.
Morton, Wm. B.,	First Class	"	1887,	£30.
Archer, James H.,	"	"	"	£30.
Lee, James,	"	"	"	£30.
Dickie, Alex. A.,	Second Class	"	"	£15.
Megaw, Robert D.,	"	"	"	£15.
Donald, Albert L.,	"	"	"	£15.
Heron, Richard C.,	First Class	"	1888,	£30.
Bradshaw, James M.,	"	"	"	£30.
Woods, William J.,	Second Class	"	"	£15.
Cochrane, John,	"	"	"	£15
M'Cracken, William J.,	"	"	"	£15.
Leathem, John G.,	First Class	"	1889,	£30.
Gillespie, James T.,	"	"	"	£30.
M'Elderry, Robert K.,	"	"	"	£30.
Fullerton, William A.,	"	"	"	£30.
Baxter, James B.,	"	"	"	£30.
Megaw, David,	Second Class	"	"	£15.
Marjoribanks, Norman E.,	"	"	"	£15.

AT FIRST UNIVERSITY EXAMINATION—con.

Name	Class		Year	Amount
Gillespie, Samuel,	Second Class	Exhibition,	1889,	£15.
Donnan, Frederick G.,	First Class	,,	1890,	£30.
Houston, William A.,	,,	,,	,,	£30.
Ashmore, Richard H.,	,,	,,	,,	£30.
M'Kitrick, Alexander,	,,	,,	,,	£30.
Porter, John A.,	Second Class	,,	,,	£15.
M'Cutcheon, Oliver E.,	,,	,,	,,	£15.
M'Mullan, Frederick,	,,	,,	,,	£15.
Bingham, Robert W.,	,,	,,	,,	£15.
Mercier, Daniel P.,	,,	,,	,,	£15.
Rowan, Marriott L.,	,,	,,	,,	£15.
Gillespie, John R.,	First Class	,,	1891,	£30.
Pyper, John,	,,	,,	,,	£30.
Woodburn, James B.,	,,	,,	,,	£30.
M'Cutcheon, Robert R.,	Second Class	,,	,,	£15.
Johnstone, Robert J.,	,,	,,	,,	£15.
Clements, Mary E.,	,,	,,	,,	£15.
Boss, Walter F.,	First Class	,,	1892,	£30.
Locke, George T.,	,,	,,	,,	£30.
Harvey, Francis W.,	,,	,,	,,	£30.
Adams, John,	,,	,,	,,	£30.
M'Calla, James,	,,	,,	,,	£30.
Miskelly, William,	,,	,,	,,	£30
Buchanan, James L.,	Second Class	,,	,,	£15
Minford, John G.,	,,	,,	,,	£15.
Clements, William T.,	,,	,,	,,	£15.
Miskelly, Samuel S.,	First Class	,,	1893,	£30
Purvis, William J.,	Second Class	,,	,,	£15.
Buchanan, Alexander C.,	,,	,,	,,	£15.
Megaw, John W. D.,	,,	,,	,,	£15
Atkinson, George C.,	,,	,,	,,	£15.
Brown, John W.,	,,	,,	,,	£15.
Rice, James,	First Class	,,	1894,	£30.
Fullerton, Joseph A.,	Second Class	,,	,,	£15.
Leathem, William H.,	,,	,,	,,	£15.
M'Neill, William,	,,	,,	,,	£15.
Todd, Ebenezer W.,	,,	,,	,,	£15.
Scott, James B.,	,,	,,	,,	£15.
Hilton, Robert,	,,	,,	,,	£15.
M'Cutcheon, Katharine S. H.,	First Class	,,	1895,	£30.
Paul, Francis J.,	,,	,,	,,	£30.
Harvey, Thomas E.,	,,	,,	,,	£30.
Porter, Samuel C.,	,,	,,	,,	£30.
Macafee, William,	,,	,,	,,	£30.
Armstrong, Frederick W.	,,	,,	,,	£30.
Minford, William,	Second Class	,,	1895,	£15.
Stoops, William A.,	,,	,,	,,	—
Hawthorne, John	,,	,,	,,	£15.
Smyth, Samuel A.,	First Class	,,	1896,	£30.
Spence, John A.,	,,	,,	,,	£30.
Stewart, Samuel E.,	Second Class	,,	,,	£15.
Wilson, George,	,,	,,	,,	£15.
Woods, James,	,,	,,	,,	£15.
Peden, Thomas U.,	,,	,,	,,	£15.
Sinclair, William T.,	,,	,,	,,	£15.
Jennings, Christian	,,	,,	,,	£15.
Vinycomb, Thomas B.,	First Class	,,	1897,	£30.
Elliott, George H.,	,,	,,	,,	£30.
Martin, James R.,	,,	,,	,,	£30.
Greer, Robert F.,	Second Class	,,	,,	£15.
Gillespie, Alfred J.,	,,	,,	,,	£15.

At First University Examination—*con.*

Waddell, John,	Second Class Exhibition,	1897,	£15.
Carnwath, Thomas,	,, ,,	,,	£15.
Malet, Christopher L.,	,, ,,	,,	£15.
Clark, Andrew,	,, ,,	,,	£15.
Adamson, Francis L.,	First Class ,,	1898,	£30.
Kerr, Hugh,	,, ,,	,,	£30.
Stoupe, Margaret,	Second Class ,,	,,	£15.
M'Donnell, John,	,, ,,	,,	£15.
Ferguson, James,	,, ,,	,,	£15.
Knox, William G.,	,, ,,	,,	£15.
Rutherford, John F.,	,, ,,	,,	£15.
M'Cullough, Reid,	,, ,,	,,	£15.

At LL.D. Examination.

Strahan, James A.,	A Prize,	1882,	£40.
Carr, William R.,	,,	,,	£25.
Watts, William N.,	,,	1883,	£25.
Hamilton, Andrew B.,	,,	1884,	£50.
Nelson, Thomas E.,	,,	,,	£25.
Harrison, Thomas,	,,	1885,	£50.
Forbes, John,	,,	,,	£25.
Turnbull, Martin H.,	,,	1886,	£25.
Gibson, Thomas H.,	,,	1889,	£21.
Johnston, William J.,	,,	1891,	£21.
Megaw, Robert D.,	,,	1892,	£42.
M'Cormick, Isaac W.,	,,	,,	£21.
Archer, James H.,	Second Class Exhibition,	1893,	£21.
M'Cutcheon, Robert R.,	First Class ,,	1898,	£42.

First Examination in Law.

Megaw, Robert D.,	A Prize,	1891,	£20.
Robb, Frederick J.,	,,	1892,	£10.
Morell, David E.,	First Class Exhibition,	1894,	£20.
M'Cutcheon, Robert B.,	Second Class ,,	1895,	£10.
Allen, David,	,, ,,	1897,	£10.

At M.D. Examination.

Donnan, William D., a Gold Medal, 1897, —

At M.Ch. Examination.

Cowden, William J., Special Prize, 1885, £20.

At M.B. Examination.

Name	Class		Year	Amount
White, William,	Second Class	Exhibition,	1884,	—
Grainger, Thomas,	〃	〃	〃	£25.
Belfern, John J.,	First Class	〃	1885,	£50.
Thomson, George S.,	Second Class	〃	1886,	£25.
Mackintosh, Henry L.,	〃	〃	1887,	£25.

At M.D., B.Ch. and B.A.O. Examinations.

Name	Class		Year	Amount
Hazlett, Robert W.,	Second Class	Exhibition,	1889,	—
Fullerton, Andrew,	First Class	〃	1890,	£40.
Campbell, Robert,	Second Class	〃	1892,	£25.
Woods, William J.,	〃	〃	1893,	£25.
Thompson, William D. T.,	〃	〃	1894,	£25.
Watt, Robert,	〃	〃	〃	£25.
Craig, James A.,	First Class	〃	1895,	£40.
Houston, Thomas,	Second Class	〃	〃	£25.
Smyth, Walter S.,	First Class	〃	1896,	£40.
Johnstone, Robert J., B.A.,	Second Class	〃	〃	£25.
M'Cully, Andrew L.,	First Class	〃	1897,	£40.
Robertson, Walter B.,	Second Class	〃	〃	£25.
M'Cay, David,	〃	〃	1898,	£25.

At Third Examination in Medicine.

Name	Class		Year	Amount
Hall, John M.,	First Class	Exhibition,	1888,	—
Griffith, Patrick G.,	Second Class	〃	1889,	—
Fullerton, Andrew,	〃	〃	〃	£20.
Woods, William J.,	First Class	〃	1891,	£30.
Jamison, Alexander,	Second Class	〃	〃	£20.
Leathem, Robert R. L.,	〃	〃	〃	£20.
M'Keown, Robert J.,	〃	〃	1892,	£20.
Watt, Robert,	〃	〃	〃	£20.
Craig, James A.,	First Class	〃	1893,	£30.
Graham, Robert A. L.,	Second Class	〃	1897,	£20.
Megaw, John W. D.,	〃	〃	〃	£20.
Hunter, William M.,	〃	〃	〃	£20.
West, John W.,	〃	〃	〃	£20.
MacIlwaine, John E.,	First Class	〃	1898,	£30.
Radcliffe, John A. D.,	Second Class	〃	〃	£20.

At Second Examination in Medicine.

Name	Class		Year	Amount
Chambers, James,	First Class	Exhibition,	1882,	—
Grainger, Thomas,	Second Class	〃	〃	£20.
M'Quitty, William B.,	First Class	〃	1883,	£40.
Buchanan, Andrew,	Second Class	〃	〃	£20.
Woods, Edmund M'N.,	〃	〃	1884,	£20.
Weatherup, William,	〃	〃	1885,	£20.
Hall, John M.,	First Class	〃	1886,	—
Fullerton, Andrew,	Second Class	〃	1888,	£15.
Robertson, Walter B.,	〃	〃	1890,	£15.
Jamison, Alex.,	〃	〃	〃	£15.
Woods, William J.,	First Class	〃	〃	£25.
Craig, James A.,	Second Class	〃	1892,	£15.
MacKeown, William J.,	First Class	〃	1893,	£25.
Beggs, Samuel T.,	Second Class	〃	〃	£15.
MacIlwaine, John E.,	〃	〃	1897,	£15.
M'Murdie, David,	〃	〃	1898,	£15.
Black, Albert L.,	〃	〃	〃	£15.

of Queen's College, Belfast.

At First Examination in Medicine.

Haslett, Robert W.,	First Class	Exhibition,	1884,	£30.
Smiley, David C.,	Second Class	,,	,,	£15.
Morton, Hamilton,	First Class	,,	1885,	£30.
Wilson, Robert,	Second Class	,,	,,	£15.
Robertson, Walter B.,	First Class	,,	1888,	£20.
Moore, Benjamin,	,,	,,	1890,	—
Houston, Thomas,	,,	,,	1891,	—
Osborne, William A.,	,,	,,	1892,	£20.
Johnstone, Robert J.,	Second Class	,,	,,	£10.
Hanna, Henry,	First Class	,,	1893,	£20.
Scott, John,	Second Class	,,	,,	£10.
M'Mordie, David,	First Class	,,	1896,	£20.
Black, Albert L.,	Second Class	,,	,,	£10.
Phillips, Walter,	,,	,,	1897,	£10.
M'Closkey, John	,,	,,	1898,	—
Johnston, Henry M.,	,,	,,	,,	£10.

At B.E. Examination.

Burden, Alexander M.,	First Class	Exhibition,	1885,	£50.
Heron, James,	A Prize,		,,	£20.
Graham, John,	Second Class	Exhibition,	1887,	£25.
Phillips, James St. J.,	,,	,,	1890,	£21.
Sides, John F.,	First Class	,,	1895,	£19.
Gailey, Thomas A.,	,,	,,	1896,	£42.
Orr, William R.,	Second Class	,,	,,	£21.

At Second Examination in Engineering.

Tate, Charles L.,	First Class	Exhibition,	1884,	£20 Prize.
Burden, Alexander M.,	,,	,,	,,	£10.
Heron, James,	Second Class	,,	,,	£20.
Anderson, Joshua T. N.,	,,	,,	1885,	£20.
Graham, John,	,,	,,	1886,	£20.
Greer, Robert T.,	,,	,,	1891,	£18.
Sides, John F.,	First Class	,,	1894,	£35.
Gailey, Thomas A.,	,,	,,	1895,	£35.

At First Examination in Engineering.

Burden, Alexander M.,	First Class	Exhibition,	1883,	£30.
Heron, James,	Second Class	,,	,,	£15.
Anderson, Joshua T. N.,	,,	,,	1884,	£15.
Graham, John,	,,	,,	1885,	£15.
Moore, Benjamin,	,,	,,	1888,	£15.
Megaw, David,	,,	,,	1892,	—
Sides, John F.,	,,	,,	1893,	£15.
Gailey, Thomas A.,	First Class	,,	1894,	£30

At Matriculation Examination.

Barnett, Richard W., Second Class Exhibition,	1881,	£12.
Gorman, William T., „ „	„	£12.
Johnston, William, „ „	„	£12
Johnson, William S., First Class „	1883,	£24.
Rowan, William H., „ „	1884,	£24.
Everett, Alice, „ „	„	£24.

Table IX.—List of Sundry Students of the College who have, since 1st January, 1881, obtained distinctions in Universities other than the Royal University of Ireland.

The date immediately following each name is that of the last Session in which the name of the Student appeared on the Roll of the College.

Eccles, John, M.A. R.U.I., M.A. Cantab. (1876–77).
1881. Wranglership, 14th place in the Mathematical Tripos, University of Cambridge.

Newsome, James C., M.A. R.U.I., B.A. T.C.D. (1876–77).
1884. Scholarship (Classical), Trinity College, Dublin.
1887. Classical Studentship, Trinity College, Dublin.

Charles, Robert H., M.A. R.U.I., M.A. T.C.D. (1877–78).
1881. Senior Moderatorship in Classics, and Junior Moderatorship in Ethics and Logics, University of Dublin.

Gorby, Thomas H., B.A. R.U.I., B.A. Cantab. (1877–78).
1881. Scholarship, Gonville and Caius College, Cambridge.

Johnston, William J., M.A. R.U.I., B.A. T.C.D. (1877–78).
1883. Senior Moderatorship in Mathematics and Physics, University of Dublin.

Wright, Almroth E., B.A., M.D. T.C.D. (1877–78).
1882. Senior Moderatorship in Modern Literature, University of Dublin.

Knowles, Thomas T., M.A. R.U.I., M.A. Cantab. (1878–79).
1882. Wranglership, 19th place in Mathematical Tripos, University of Cambridge.

Shaver, Richard W., M.A. R.U.I., B.A. T.C.D. (1879–80).
1881. Scholarship (Classical), University of Dublin.
1883. Senior Moderatorship in Ethics and Logics, and Junior Moderatorship in Classics, University of Dublin.

Reid, James S., B.A. R.U.I. (1880–81).
1882. Foundation Scholarship, Lincoln College, Oxford.

M'Farland, Robert A. H., M.A. R.U.I., B.A. Cantab. (1880–81).
1882. Scholarship, Gonville and Caius College, Cambridge.
1883. Wranglership, 9th place in Mathematical Tripos, University of Cambridge.
„ Exhibition, Gonville and Caius College, Cambridge.

Semple, Robert H., M.A. R.U.I., B.A. Cantab. (1880–81).
1881. Sizarship, St. John's College, Cambridge.
„ Exhibition, Goldsmiths' Company, University of Cambridge.
„ Exhibition at First B.A. Examination in Mathematics, University of London.

ANDERSON, WILLIAM C. F., B.A. R.U.I., B.A. Durham (1881–82).
1882. Foundation Scholarship, University of Durham.
" Newby Scholarship, University of Durham.
1883. First Year Scholarship, University of Durham.
" University Classical Scholarship, University of Durham.
1884. Gabbet Prize for Essay on Moral Philosophy, University of Durham.
Adam de Brome Exhibition, Oriel College, Oxford.
1885. Second Class in Classical Moderations, University of Oxford.
1887. Second Class in Final Classical School, University of Oxford.

LARMOR, ALEXANDER, M.A. R.U.I., M.A. Cantab. (1881–82).
1881. First Entrance Scholarship in Mathematics, Clare College, Cambridge.
1882. Foundation Scholarship, Clare College, Cambridge.
1884. Wranglership, 11th place in Mathematical Tripos, University of Cambridge.
1885. Berkeley Fellowship, Owens College, Manchester.
Fellowship, Clare College, Cambridge.

CAMPBELL, ALBERT, B.A. Cantab. (1882–83).
1884. Foundation Scholarship, Corpus Christi College, Cambridge.
1885. First Senior Optime, University of Cambridge.

M'VICKER, JOHN W., B.A. R.U.I. (1882–83).
1883. Exhibition in Mathematics, Worcester College, Oxford.

STEWART, DAVID A., B.A. R.U.I., M.A. Cantab. (1882–83).
1881. First Mathematical Scholarship, Caius College, Cambridge.
1883. Foundation Scholarship, Caius College, Cambridge.
" Mathematical Scholarship, University of London.
" Goldsmith Exhibition, University of Cambridge.

RUSSELL, WILLIAM A., B.A. R.U.I., B.A. Cantab. (1883–84).
1883. Exhibition, St. John's College, Cambridge.
" Sizarship, St. John's College, Cambridge.
1885. Goldsmith Exhibition, University of Cambridge.
1886. Honours in Classical Tripos, University of Cambridge.

CAMPBELL, JOHN E., M.A. R.U.I., M.A. Oxon. (1883–84).
1883. Mathematical Scholarship, Hertford College, Oxford.
1885. Junior University Mathematical Scholarship, and First Class in Mathematical Moderations, University of Oxford.
1887. First Class in Final Mathematical School, University of Oxford.
1887. Fellowship, Hertford College, Oxford.
1888. Senior Mathematical Scholarship, University of Oxford.

DARBISHIRE, HERBERT D., B.A. R.U.I., M.A. Cantab. (1883–84).
1883. Sizarship, St. John's College, Cambridge.
1885. Honours in Classical Tripos, University of Cambridge.
1888. Foundation Scholarship, St. John's College, Cambridge.
1889. M'Mahon Law Scholarship, St. John's College, Cambridge.
1892. Fellowship, St. John's College, Cambridge.

BARNETT, RICHARD W., B.CH., M.A., B.C.L. Oxon. (1881–82).
1885. Third Class in Classical Moderations, University of Oxford.
1887. Second Class in Jurisprudence, University of Oxford.

ORR, WILLIAM M'F., M.A. R.U.I., M.A. Cantab. (1881–85).
1884. Foundation Scholarship, St John's College, Cambridge.
1886. Exhibition in St. John's College, Cambridge.
1888. Senior Wrangler in Mathematical Tripos, University of Cambridge.
1889. First Class in Mathematical Tripos, Part II.

TATE, JAMES, M.A. R.U.I., B.A. Cantab. (1883–84).
1886. Sixteenth Wrangler, University of Cambridge.
1886. Foundation Scholarship, St. John's College, Cambridge.

STEEDE, BENJAMIN H., M.D. T.C.D. (1885–86).
1886. Science Scholarship, Trinity College, Dublin.
1887. Mathematical Studentship, Trinity College, Dublin.
1889. Bishop Law Mathematical Premium, Trinity College, Dublin.

PORTER, WILLIAM H., B.A. Oxford (1885–86).
1887. Scholarship, Lincoln College, Oxford.
1888. Goldsmith Exhibition, University of Oxford.
1889. Second Class in Classical Moderations, University of Oxford.
1891. Second Class in Final Classical School, University of Oxford.
1893. Chancellor's Prize for English Prose Essay, University of Oxford.

GREGG, JAMES, M.A. R.U.I., M.A. T.C.D. (1880–81).
1888. First Science Scholarship, Trinity College, Dublin.

LUKE, EDWARD H., B.A. R.U.I. (1886–87).
1888. Classical Scholarship, Trinity College, Dublin.

MAJOR, HAROLD W., B.A. R.U.I., B.A. Cantab. (1887–88).
1888. First Entrance Scholarship in Mathematics, Queen's College, Cambridge.
1889. Foundation Scholarship in Mathematics, Queen's College, Cambridge.
1891. Second Class Honours in Mathematical Tripos, University of Cambridge.

M'BRIDE, ERNEST W., M.A. Cantab., D.Sc. Lond. (1887–88).
1888. Entrance Exhibition, St. John's College, Cambridge.
1889. Exhibition in Natural Science, St. John's College, Cambridge.
1890. B.Sc. with First Class Honours and Exhibition in Natural Science, University of London.
„ First Class Honours at Natural Science Tripos, Part I., University of Cambridge.
„ Foundation Scholarship, St. John's College, Cambridge.
1891. First Class Honours in Natural Science Tripos, Part II. University of Cambridge.
„ Hughes Prize, St. John's College, Cambridge.
1892. Appointed Demonstrator in Natural Science at University of Cambridge.
1893. Fellowship, St. John's College, Cambridge.
„ The Walsingham Medal for original work in Natural Science, University of Cambridge.

HASLETT, WILLIAM W., B.A. R.U.I., M.A. Cantab. (1888–89).
1888. Entrance Exhibition, St. John's College, Cambridge.
1890. Foundation Scholarship, St. John's College, Cambridge.
1891. First Class Honours in Classical Tripos, Part I. University of Cambridge.
1893. First Class Honours in Classical Tripos, Part II., University of Cambridge.

MONTGOMERY, ROBERT, M.A. R.U.I., B.A. Cantab. (1887–88).
 1889. Foundation Sizarship, and First Class Honours in Classics, Trinity College, Cambridge.
 1890. Foundation Scholarship, Trinity College, Cambridge.
 1891. First Class Honours in Classical Tripos, University of Cambridge.

ALEXANDER, JOHN J., M.A. R.U.I., B.A. Cantab. (1887–88).
 1887. Entrance Exhibition, St. John's College, Cambridge.
 1889. Foundation Scholarship, St. John's College, Cambridge.
 1890. Wranglership, Seventh place in Mathematical Tripos, University of Cambridge.

LEE, JAMES, B.A. R.U.I. (1888–89).
 1889. Entrance Exhibition, St. John's College, Cambridge.

MORTON, WILLIAM B., M.A. R.U.I., M.A. Cantab. (1888–89).
 1889. Entrance Exhibition, St. John's College, Cambridge.
 1891. Foundation Scholarship, St. John's College, Cambridge.
 1892. Wranglership, Eighth place in Mathematical Tripos, University of Cambridge.

COTTER, WILLIAM K. P., B.A. R.U.I., M.A. T.C.D. (1888–89).
 1888. Classical Scholarship, Trinity College, Dublin.

HERON, RICHARD C., B.A. R.U.I., B.A. Cantab. (1889–90).
 1889. Exhibition, St. John's College, Cambridge.
 1891. Goldsmith Exhibition, University of Cambridge.
 " Foundation Sizarship, St. John's College, Cambridge.
 1892. Foundation Scholarship, St. John's College, Cambridge.
 1893. Wranglership, Twentieth place in Mathematical Tripos, University of Cambridge.

STEWART, JAMES A., B.A. R.U.I. (1888–89).
 1889. Exhibition, St. John's College, Cambridge.
 1891. Foundation Scholarship, St. John's College, Cambridge.

KNIGHTLEY, FREDERICK B., B.A. R.U.I., B.A. Cantab. (1886–7).
 1890. Third Class Honours in Historical Tripos, University of Cambridge.

LEATHEM, JOHN G., M.A. R.U.I., M.A. Cantab. (1890–91).
 1891. Entrance Exhibition, St. John's College, Cambridge.
 1894. Hughes Prize, St. John's College, Cambridge.
 " Wranglership, Fourth place in Mathematical Tripos, University of Cambridge.
 1895. First Division of First Class in Mathematical Tripos, Part II., University of Cambridge.
 " Sir Isaac Newton Studentship, University of Cambridge.
 1898. Fellowship, St. John's College, Cambridge.

M'ELDERRY, ROBERT K., M.A. R.U.I., B.A. Cantab. (1890–91).
 1891. Entrance Exhibition, St. John's College, Cambridge.
 1893. Hughes Prize, St. John's College, Cambridge.
 1894. First Class, 2nd Division, in Classical Tripos, Part I., University of Cambridge.
 1895. First Class in Classical Tripos, Part II., University of Cambridge, with Star for distinguished answering in History Section.
 1897. Fellowship, St. John's College, Cambridge.

M'VICKER, CHARLES EDWARD, B.A. Cantab., M.A. T.C.D. (1881–82).
1893. Wranglership, Seventeenth place in Mathematical Tripos, University of Cambridge.

BOAS, WALTER P., B.A. R.U.I. (1891–93).
1892. Entrance Exhibition, St. John's College, Cambridge.
1894. Exhibition, St. John's College, Cambridge.

HOUSTON, WILLIAM A., M.A. R.U.I., B.A. Cantab. (1891–92).
1892. Entrance Exhibition, St. John's College, Cambridge.
1894. Foundation Scholarship, St. John's College, Cambridge.
1896. Wranglership, Fifth place in Mathematical Tripos, University of Cambridge.
1897. First Class, First Division, in Mathematical Tripos, Part II., University of Cambridge.
1898. Second Smith's Prize.

LOGAN, GEORGE T., B.A. R.U.I., B.A. Cantab. (1893–94).
1894. Entrance Exhibition, St. John's College, Cambridge. Foundation Scholarship, St. John's College, Cambridge.
1897. Honours in Mathematical Tripos, Part I., University of Cambridge.

ROBB, ALFRED A., B.A. R.U.I., B.A. Cantab. (1893–94).
1894. Entrance Exhibition, St. John's College, Cambridge.
1897. Honours in Mathematical Tripos, Part I., University of Cambridge.

CLEMENTS, WILLIAM T., B.A. Cantab. (1893–94).
1894. Entrance Exhibition, St. John's College, Cambridge.
1897. Honours in Mathematical Tripos, Part I., University of Cambridge.

BAXTER, JAMES SINCLAIR, B.A. R.U.I., LL.B. London (1893–94).
1894. LL.B. with First Class Honours, London University.

MEGAW, ROBERT D., B.A., LL.B. R.U.I. (1892–93).
1894. Prize of £50 for distinguished answering at the Examination for the Reid Professorship, Trinity College, Dublin.

RICE, JAMES, B.A. R.U.I. (1895–96).
1894. Entrance Exhibition, St. John's College, Cambridge.

REID, DAVID D., B.A. Oxon. (1892–93).
Scholarship in History, New College, Oxford.
1896. First Class in Modern History Class List, University of Oxford.
1897. Second Class in School of Jurisprudence, University of Oxford.

ARMSTRONG, FREDERICK W., B.A. R.U.I. (1896–97).
1897. Exhibition in Classics of £50 at Entrance Scholarship Examination, St. John's College, Cambridge.

EVERETT, ALEXANDER FRASER (1896–97).
1899. Exhibition in History, New College, Oxford, £50 per annum during residence.

STEWART-WALLACE, JOHN S. (1894–95).
1899. First Class, Final Honour School of Jurisprudence, University of Oxford.

Table X.—Benefactors of Queen's College, Belfast, since its Foundation in 1845.

Anno.

1847. Presented by Charles Davis, Esq., a large oil painting of the Assassination of Peter the Martyr, by Atkins, being a copy of the original painting by Titian.

—— Presented by Professor Craik, a portrait of Confucius.

1851. The Governors of the Armagh Observatory, with the sanction of Her Majesty, transferred to the College the Transit Instrument and Astronomical Clock which were formerly in the Observatory at Kew.

The Lords of the Admiralty, on the recommendation of the Astronomer Royal of England, acceded to an application from Professor Wilson for transferring to the College a Mural Circle by Jones, which had been in use at the Cape of Good Hope.

For the reception of these instruments an Observatory was erected on the College grounds, the expense having been defrayed by subscription.

1854. Presented by W. P. Wilson, Esq., M.A., former Professor of Mathematics in the College, a Bust of Sir Isaac Newton.

1855. Presented by Robert Lyon, Esq., London, an oil portrait of James the First of England when a child, an oil portrait of Jonanes Carolus, and an oil portrait of John Milton.

1860. An oil portrait of Hugh Carlisle, M.D., former Professor of Anatomy and Physiology in the College; presented by the subscribers.

1864. Given by R. M. Wilson, Esq., an Exhibition of Twenty Pounds to be conferred annually upon one or more of the most deserving unsuccessful candidates for a Scholarship of the First Year.

This Exhibition was awarded for eleven years.

1861. Given by the Royal Academical Institution, Belfast, two Exhibitions of Five Pounds each, to be conferred annually upon students from that Institution who obtain the highest places in the Literary and Science Divisions, at the Examination for Scholarships of the First Year.

1866. Given by John Charters, Esq., an Exhibition, value Fifteen Pounds, and two Exhibitions, value Ten Pounds each, in the Literary Division of the Faculty of Arts; also one Exhibition, value Fifteen Pounds, and two, value Ten Pounds each, in the Science Division of the Faculty of Arts, to be called the "Charters' Exhibitions," and to be annually awarded during ten years, at the Examinations for the Literary and Scientific Scholarships of the first year, to students who, during at least one year previous to their entrance into college, were in continuous attendance at the Royal Academical Institution, and who attain the standard of excellence required at the Junior Scholarship Examinations. Also, an Exhibition, value Fifty Pounds, tenable for one year, to be called the "Charters' Medical Exhibition," to be annually awarded during ten years, in connexion with the Belfast School of Medicine, by the Trustees of the "Charters' Educational Fund."

—— An oil portrait of William Burden, M.D., former Professor of Midwifery in the College; presented by the subscribers.

1868. Bequeathed by Robert Sullivan, Esq., LL.D., Barrister-at-Law, the sum of Four Thousand Pounds for the endowment of Three Scholarships in Queen's College, Belfast, to be called the Sullivan Scholarships, two of them to be restricted to candidates who shall have acted as Teachers or Assistant Teachers in Irish National Schools for at least two years, and one of them to candidates who shall have been educated in the Royal Academical Institution, Belfast, for at least three years.

These Scholarships are of the annual value of Forty Pounds each and are tenable for three years.

Anno.

1869. Given by William Coates, Esq., a prize, value Thirty Pounds, to be called "The Coates Prize," and to be awarded in the Department of Engineering.

This prize was awarded for four years.

1869. A Bust of the Rev. P. Shuldham Henry, D.D., late President of the College, presented by the Professors and other subscribers.

1871. An oil portrait of George L. Craik, LL.D., former Professor of History and English Literature in the College, and also a photograph group of some of the Professors; presented by Messrs. Marcus Ward & Co.

1871. Bequeathed by John Porter, Esq., the sum of Three Thousand One Hundred and Ten Pounds Eight Shillings and Four Pence for the endowment of Two Scholarships in Queen's College, Belfast, to be called "The Porter Scholarships." These scholarships are of the annual value of Fifty Pounds each, and are tenable for two years.

1873. A deed was executed by William Dunville, Esq., establishing the "Sorella Trust." This deed, which also provides funds for other educational purposes not connected with the College, endows two Studentships in Queen's College, Belfast, to be called "The Dunville Studentships." They are awarded, in alternate years, one, for the encouragement of the study of Mathematical and Physical Science, the other, for the encouragement of the study of Natural Science. Each person obtaining a Studentship receives £45 for the first year, and £100 for the second year.

1873. Given by the Widow and Children of the late John Robinson M'Clean, Esq., Civil Engineer, London, through the hands of the Rev. P. S. Henry, D.D., President, the sum of Five Hundred Pounds, to be expended in the purchase of Scientific works for the Library of Queen's College, Belfast.

1874. Given by the Methodist College, Belfast, one Exhibition, value Ten Pounds, to be awarded annually to the highest answerer among students from the Methodist College who obtain Literary Scholarships of the first year in Queen's College, Belfast; and another Exhibition, also value Ten Pounds, to the highest answerer among students from the Methodist College, who obtain Science Scholarships of the First Year in the same College.

1876. Given by the Reverend Arthur Hercules Pakenham, for the endowment of two Scholarships in Queen's College, Belfast, one to be called the "Sir Hercules Pakenham Scholarship," and the other the "Emily Lady Pakenham Scholarship," the sum of One Thousand Pounds, invested in five bonds of £100 each of the Moscow Jaroslaw Railway Company, and five bonds of £100 each of the Charkoff Azov Railway Company.

1877. Given by an anonymous donor, Ten Pounds, to provide for an Entrance Prize of Five Pounds, to be awarded for proficiency in French.

This prize was awarded for two years.

1878. An oil portrait of Alexander Gordon, M.D., former Professor of Surgery in the College; presented by the subscribers.

1880. The subscribers to a testimonial given to Dr. MacDonell on his retirement from the Professorship of Greek, presented to the College, in addition to a portrait of Dr. MacDonell now placed in the Examination Hall, a collection of Classical and Oriental Works of the value of £275, selected from the library of Dr. MacDonell, to form the nucleus of a department of the Library to be called "The MacDonell Library."

Anno.

1881. The sum of One Thousand Seven Hundred and Ninety-two Pounds Seven Shillings was raised by public subscription, for the establishment of a Scholarship to commemorate the distinguished services, rendered to this College and to Chemical Science, by Dr. Thomas Andrews, F.R.S., the late Vice-President.

At the same time a full-length Oil Portrait of Dr. Andrews was placed in the Examination Hall.

1882. The sum of Eight Hundred and Seventy-five Pounds Six Shillings, in New Three per Cent. Government Stock, being a portion of the bequest of the late Lord Blayney, was transferred to this College by the Queen's University.

1882. A Medal, to be awarded annually, was founded with a portion of the residue of the Peel Fund of the late Queen's University.

1882. An Oil Portrait of William Nesbitt, M.A., former Professor of Lane in the College; presented by the Subscribers.

1889. Bequeathed by John M'Kane, Esq., LL.D., Barrister-at-Law, former Professor of English Law in the College, a Gold Medal to be awarded annually for answering in Jurisprudence and Political Economy.

1889. An Oil Portrait of the Rev. J. Leslie Porter, D.D., LL.D., late President of the College; presented by the Presidents and Professors.

1890. An Oil Portrait of John Purser, LL.D., Professor of Mathematics in the College; presented by his former students.

1891. Given by Her Majesty's Commissioners of the Exhibition of 1851 the nomination to a Scholarship of the value of £150 per annum, tenable for two, or, under special conditions, for three years, and limited to those branches of Science (such as Physics, Mechanics, and Chemistry), the extension of which is specially important for our national industries.

1893. Given by Her Majesty's Commissioners of the Exhibition of 1851 the nomination to a Scholarship of the value of £150 per annum, tenable for two, or, under special conditions, for three years, as above.

1893. Founded by the Trustees of the Sorella Trust the "Dunville Chair of Physiology."

1894. An Oil Portrait of Peter Redfern, M.D., Professor of Anatomy and Physiology 1860–93; presented by the Subscribers.

1894. Subscribed, and raised by a Fancy Fair, about £8,000 for the erection of a College Union.

1895. Given by Her Majesty's Commissioners of the Exhibition of 1851 the nomination to a Scholarship of the value of £150 per annum, tenable for two, or, under special conditions, for three years, as above.

1895. An Oil Painting of James MacAdam, Esq., the first Librarian of the College, presented by Miss MacAdam.

1896. Given by the Trustees of the Sorella Trust the sum of £100 for the purchase of apparatus for the department of Physiology.

1897. Given by Her Majesty's Commissioners of the Exhibition of 1851 the nomination to a Scholarship of the value of £150 per annum, tenable for two, or, under special conditions, for three years, as above.

1897. An Oil Portrait of the Rev. George Hill, Librarian of the College, 1850–1880; presented by the Subscribers.

1897. An Oil Portrait of Sir William MacCormac, Bart., M.D., President of the Royal College of Surgeons, England; presented by the Subscribers.

1897. An Oil Portrait of John Stevelly, LL.D., Professor of Natural Philosophy, 1849–1867; presented by his son, Robert Sankey Stevelly, M.A.

1898. Two Friends, to assist in the Establishment of a Museum of Sanitary Science, £20.

1898. An Oil Portrait of Joseph David Everett, M.A., D.C.L., F.R.S., Professor of Natural Philosophy, 1867–1898; presented by the Subscribers.

1899. Given by Her Majesty's Commissioners of the Exhibition of 1851 the nomination to a Scholarship of the value of £150 per annum, tenable for two, or, under special conditions, for three years, as above.

1899. Two Friends, to assist in general equipment of the College, £20.

Donations to the Library, 1898–99.

Donations.	Presented.
P. E. Huschke, Jurisprudentiae Antejustinianae quae supersunt.	By Mr. Thomas Andrews.
Charles C. Coe, Nature versus Natural Selection, an Essay on Organic Evolution.	By the Author.
Mittheilungen der Medicinischen Fakultät zu Tokio, Vol. IV.	By the University.
Annotationes Zoologicae Japonenses, 3 parts.	By the University of Tokio.
University of Toronto Studies.	By the University.
Wachsmuth and Springer, North American Crinoidea.	By the Keepers of the Museum of Harvard College.
The Kansas University Quarterly.	By the University.
Year Book of the Department of Agriculture, U.S.A.	By the Department.
S. Shannon Millin, Petty Sessions Digest.	By the Author.
Annals of the Royal Botanic Gardens, Calcutta, Vol. VIII., Parts 1–4.	By His Honour the Lieut.-General of Bengal.

Donations.	Presented.
P. O. Schjott, Samlede Philologiske Afhandlinger.	By the University of Christiania.
Fowler, J. K., and R. J. Godlee, Diseases of the Lungs.	By Professor Symington.
Extracts from the Private Letters of Sir William Fothergill Cooke.	By Professor John Perry.
The Book of Ayub, translated by R. Sadler.	By the Translator.
The Apocalypse of St. John, translated by the Rev. R. Sadler.	By the Translator.
Memorial Book of the Sesquicentennial Celebration of the Founding of the College of New Jersey, and of the Ceremonies inaugurating Princeton University	By the President and Trustees of the Faculty of Princeton University.
Index Catalogue of the Library of the Surgeon-General, U. S. Army, Vol. III.	By the Librarian.
Peter Tait, Scientific Papers, Vol. I.	By the Syndics of the University Press, Cambridge.
Proceedings of the U.S.A. National Museum, New Series, beginning with Vol. XIX.	By the Trustees of the Museum.
W. A. Browne, The Money Weights and Measures of the Chief Commercial Nations.	By the Author.
Geological Map of *Europe*.	By the Royal Society of London.
William M'Keown, A Treatise on Unripe Cataract.	By the Author.
Report of the Meeting of the British Association, 1898.	By the Association.
C. P. Tiele, Elements of the Science of Religion, Vol. II.	By the Senatus Academicus, Edinburgh.
S. Squire Sprigge, The Life and Times of Thomas Wakley.	By his Son, Thomas Wakley, Junior.
Catalogue Méthodique des Imprimés de la Bibliothèque Publique de Douai: (1.) Sciences; (2.) Histoire de France.	By the Conseil Municipal de la ville de Douai.
Charles Janet, Nine Pamphlets on Bees, Wasps, and Ants (in French).	By the Author.
S. M'Kinney, The Origin and Nature of Man. (Two copies.)	By the Author.
Thomas K. Monro, History of the Chronic Degenerative Diseases of the Central Nervous System.	By the Author.
Clement E. Pike, An Account of the Life of Robert Cunningham, Minister of Holywood.	By the Author.

Donations.	Presented.
Charles P. Reichel, sometime Bishop of Meath, Sermons.	By his Son, H. R. Reichel, Principal of the University College of North Wales.
The Journal of Balneology.	By the Editors and Publishers.
David H. Hoppe, Ectypa Plantarum Ratisbonensium. Three volumes of Botanical Plates, Nature—printed by Seligmann's process.	By Mrs. Robert Lindsay.

The following Institutions have continued to present their publications:—

The Royal Irish Academy.
The British Museum.
The Government of India.
" " China (Customs).
" " Canada (Geological Survey).
" " Norway (North Pole Expedition).
The Cambridge Philosophical Society.
The Philosophical Society, Birmingham.
The Institute of Civil Engineers.
The South Kensington Museum.
The Smithsonian Institution.
The Bureau of Education, Washington.
The U. S. Department of Agriculture.
Messrs. Macmillan & Co. and Messrs. Williams & Norgate presented copies of numerous Educational Publications.

The following Universities and Colleges presented their Calendars:—

The University of Edinburgh.
" " Glasgow.
" " Aberdeen.
" " St. Andrews.
" " Durham.
" " Wales.
Victoria University.
Royal University of Ireland.
The University of Melbourne.
" " Sydney.
" " Princeton.
" " Chicago.
" " Michigan.
" " California.
Owens College, Manchester.
Queen's College, Birmingham.
Mason College, Birmingham.
University College, Bristol.
The Yorkshire College, Leeds.
University College, Nottingham.
University College, Aberystwith.
Royal Holloway College.
Anderson's College, Glasgow.
University College, Dundee.
The College of Medicine, Newcastle-on-Tyne.
Queen's College, Cork.
Queen's College, Galway.
Register of the University of Chicago.

DONATIONS TO THE NATURAL HISTORY MUSEUM.

A considerable number of donations have been received from friends, among which the following may be mentioned:—

Bear and Fox, presented by David Walker, esq., M.D., a former student of the College.

Collection of Shells presented by Mrs. M'Gee, widow of the late Dr. M'Gee.

Casts and specimens of extinct animals, presented by the Earl of Enniskillen.

Five very rare Birds from Yarkand, presented by Dr. Scully, Indian Medical Service.

Collections of Japanese Birds, prepared and presented by Dr. S. Campbell, Fleet Surgeon, R.N.

Collections of Animals, chiefly Marine, from the East Coast of Africa and Zulu Archipelago, presented by Lieut. Dixon, R.N.

Miscellaneous specimens, presented by Staff-Surgeon W. Anderson, R.N., a former student of the College.

Large collection of Indian birds, some of considerable rarity, presented on various occasions by Dr. Cunningham, Professor of Physiology, Medical College, Calcutta.

Specimens of North American birds and Irish fishes, presented by G. D. Ogilby, esq., a student of the College.

Collection of Animals and Minerals from Australia, presented by Edward Leslie Pooler, esq., M.D., a former student of the College.

Collection of Animals from the New Hebrides, &c., presented by James Dunlop, esq., M.D., Surgeon R.N., a former student of the College.

Collection of Animals from Sumatra, presented by John B. Graham, esq., M.D., a former student of the College.

Collection of Birds from the Himalayas, presented by Alexander Porter, esq., M.D., Brigade Surgeon, H.M. Indian Army, a former student of the College.

Collection of Reptiles from South Australia, presented by Edward Leslie Pooler, esq., M.D., a former student of the College.

Very fine specimen of *Goliathus Druryi* from West Africa, presented by R. J. M'Keown, esq., M.B., a former student of the College.

Two fine specimens of the remarkable New Zealand lizard, *Sphenodon*, presented by James Young, esq., M.D., New Zealand, a former student of the College

A fine specimen of *Manis longicaudata*, and a queen Termite or White Ant, presented by Captain R. A. L. Irvine.

A collection of dried plants and other objects from Ulster, presented by Hugh Hyndman, esq., LL.D., a former student of the College.

A fine skull of Hippopotamus, presented by George Gray, esq., M.D., J.P., Newcastle, co. Down, a former student of the College.

A collection of Botanical specimens, presented by Henry Hanna, esq., M.A., B.SC., Demonstrator of Botany and Palæontology, Royal College of Science, Dublin.

A curious small Shark (Euprotomicrus Labordii), obtained by Captain Paley of the ship "Mawhan," and presented to the Museum through the medium of Mr. Adam T. Barkley, Belfast.

DONATIONS TO THE MEDICAL MUSEUMS

A beautiful series of microscopical preparations, showing the texture of many organs of the body, was presented by Dr. Thiersch, of Leipzic, to Dr. Redfern, Professor of Anatomy, and by him generously handed over to the College.

A series of 30 slides, containing embryological sections prepared under his personal superintendence, was presented by Professor Kölliker to Dr. Redfern, and by him to the College.

A fine collection of over 200 vesical calculi removed by surgical operation in India by Surgeon-Major J. A. Cunningham, Indian Medical Service, a former student of the College, and presented by him.

A very large collection of specimens, formerly in Minto House, Edinburgh, presented by Professor Symington.

Various specimens presented by Professor Symington, M.D.; Professor Byers, M.D.; Professor Sinclair, M.D.; Dr. J. Lorrain Smith, Dr. G. St. George, Dr. H. R. Irwin, and Dr. W. M. Elliott.

TABLE XI.—LIST of the PROFESSORS and OFFICERS of the COLLEGE, showing their length of Service, their Salaries, and their Emoluments from Class Fees.

—		Appointed.	Salary.			Class Fees for year ended 31st March, 18[illegible].			Total.		
			£	s.	d.	£	s.	d.	£	s.	d.
	PROFESSORS.										
Greek,	Samuel Dill, M.A.,	27 February, 1890,	312	0	0	101	0	0	413	0	0
Latin,	Thomas William Dougan, M.A.,	7 January, 1882,	312	0	0	139	0	0	451	0	0
Mathematics,	John Purser, LL.D., D.SC., F.R.U.I.,	8 July, 1863,	312	0	0	101	0	0	413	0	0
Natural Philosophy,	William Blair Morton, M.A., F.R.U.I.,	30 March, 1897,	312	0	0	215	0	0	527	0	0
History and English Literature,	Samuel James MacMullan, M.A., F.R.U.I.,	15 January, 1889,	312	0	0	105	0	0	417	0	0
Logic and Metaphysics,	John Park, M.A., D.LIT., F.R.U.I.,	1 October, 1868,	312	0	0	108	0	0	420	0	0
Chemistry,	Edmund Albert Letts, PH.D., F.R.S.E., F.R.U.I.,	4 December, 1879,	282	0	0	347	10	0	629	10	0
Natural History,	Robert O. Cunningham, M.D., F.L.S., F.G.S., F.R.U.I.	5 April, 1871,	283	0	0	154	0	0	437	0	0
Modern Languages,	Albert Ludwig Meissner, PH.D.,	6 October, 1865,	202	0	0	43	0	0	245	0	0
Jurisprudence and Political Economy,	William Graham, M.A.,	14 June, 1882,	150	0	0	59	0	0	209	0	0
English Law,	James Andrew Strahan, LL.B.,	14 January, 1886,	147	19	3	—			147	19	3
	William Newell Watts, LL.D.,	28 February, 1889,	—			28	0	0	28	0	0
Anatomy,	Johnson Symington, M.D., F.R.S.E., F.R.U.I.	10 October, 1893,	193	0	0	481	18	0	674	18	0
Physiology,	William Henry Thompson, M.D., F.R.C.S., Eng.,	10 October, 1893,	*250	0	0	299	0	0	549	0	0
Medicine,	James Cuming, M.A., M.D., F.K.Q.C.P.	26 August, 1865,	120	0	0	71	0	0	191	0	0
Surgery,	Thomas Sinclair, M.D., M.CH., F.R.C.S., Eng.,	1 November, 1886,	120	0	0	133	0	0	253	0	0
Materia Medica,	William Whitla, M.A., M.D.,	23 October, 1890,	120	0	0	66	0	0	186	0	0
Midwifery,	John William Byers, M.A., M.D., M.A.O.,	30 September, 1893,	120	0	0	64	0	0	184	0	0
Civil Engineering,	Maurice Frederick FitzGerald, B.A., Assoc. M.I.C.E.	29 November, 1884,	230	0	0	81	0	0	311	0	0
Agriculture,	John Frederick Hodges, M.D., F.C.S., F.I.C.	4 August, 1849,	150	0	0	—			150	0	0
	OFFICERS.										
Registrar,	John Purser, LL.D.,	8 January, 1878,	75	0	0	—			75	0	0
Bursar,	William Wylie,	5 December, 1894,	150	0	0	—			150	0	0
Librarian,	Albert Ludwig Meissner, PH.D.,	4 July, 1883,	75	0	0	—			75	0	0

* Of this sum £240 is paid by the Trustees of the "Dunville Trust," who have endowed the Dunville Chair of Physiology with that annual amount.

TABLE XII.—ACCOUNT OF THE RECEIPTS AND EXPENDITURE OF

RECEIPTS.		£ s. d.
Balance on 1st April, 1858, viz.:—		
General Account,	£638 5 11	
Library Deposits,	418 0 0	
Private Endowment Accounts,	707 0 11	
		1,763 16 10
Permanent Grant charged on the Consolidated Fund,	£7,000 0 0	
Less Income Tax	164 18 4	
		6,835 0 0
Annual Parliamentary Grant in Aid of Augmentation of Professors' Salaries,	£140 0 0	
Less Income Tax,	6 0 0	
		134 0 0
Annual Parliamentary Grant in Aid of Expenses of Maintenance,		1,600 0 0
College Fees, viz.:—		
261 at 13s.,	£170 19 0	
9 at 2s. (for use of Library),	0 18 0	
One Matriculation Fee,	0 10 0	
Calendars sold,	1 7 0	
Proportion of Practical Pharmacy fees in aid of expenses of class: 76 at 15s.,	56 0 0	
		191 17 0
Miscellaneous:—		
Dividends from Government Stock,	£17 13 5	
Interest from Bank,	15 11 0	
Donation from Two Anonymous Friends to assist in establishing a Museum of Sanitary Science,	20 0 0	
		53 4 5
Dunville Chair of Physiology:—Private Endowment,	£180 0 0	
Less Income Tax,	6 0 0	
		174 0 0
Professors' Class Fees,		2,140 0 0
Lecturers' Class Fees,		378 0 0
Library Deposits,		53 0 0
Private Endowment Scholarships,		107 16 1
		£10,611 1 5

THE COLLEGE IN THE YEAR ENDING 31st MARCH, 1899.

PAYMENTS.			£ s. d.
Permanent Grant:—			
Salaries of President, Professors, and Officers,	£4,997 19 3		
Less Income Tax,	161 12 0		
		£4,816 7 3	
Salaries of Minor Officers and Servants,	£400 0 0		
Less Income Tax,	3 0 0		
		497 0 0	
Scholarships and Prizes,		1,358 18 4	
Salary of Lecturer in Pathology,		50 0 0	
Salary of [illegible] for Chair of English Law,		26 3 4	
			6,744 8 7
Special Grant:—Augmentation of Professors' Salaries,		150 0 0	
Less Income Tax,		5 0 0	
			145 0 0
Expenditure under Annual Parliamentary Grant, College Fees, and Miscellaneous Receipts:—			
Maintenance of Library and Museums, Departmental and General Expenses, viz.:—			
Library:—			
Ancient and Modern Languages,	£76 6 7		
Mathematical and Physical Sciences,	39 19 7		
Natural Sciences,	58 5 9		
Engineering,	6 1 9		
Medical Sciences,	155 7 8		
Mental and Legal Sciences,	37 16 7		
General Department,	4 4 10		
Binding,	67 19 0		
		494 4 10	
Laboratories:—			
Chemical Laboratory,	£74 3 9		
Physical Cabinet,	58 10 6		
Engineering,	6 19 3		
Medical Faculty,	155 1 3		
		314 14 9	
Museums,		69 9 0	
Printing, Stationery, and Advertising,		148 9 10	
Heating and Lighting,		795 4 11	
Botanic Garden and College Grounds,		197 11 1	
Miscellaneous, viz.:—			
Porters' Clothing,	£31 10 0		
Water Supply,	77 6 8		
Additional Salaries of Porters,	60 13 6		
Incidental Expenses,	116 9 4		
		355 14 4	
			1,879 16 11
Dunville Chair of Physiology:—			
Salary of Professor,		260 0 0	
Less Income Tax,		9 0 0	
			251 0 0
Class Fees paid to Professors,			2,340 0 0
Class Fees paid to Lecturers,			276 0 0
Library Deposits,			81 0 0
Private Endowment Scholarships,			991 16 4
Physiological and Pathological Laboratories,			85 1 10
Fittings and Equipment of Medical Museum,			90 9 7
Balance on 31st March, 1899, viz.:—			
General Account,		£876 6 10	
Library Deposits,		190 0 0	
Private Endowment Accounts,		903 0 4	
			1,306 13 6
			£15,011 1 6

www.ingramcontent.com/pod-product-compliance
Lightning Source LLC
Chambersburg PA
CBHW021541270326
41930CB00008B/1329
* 9 7 8 3 7 4 2 8 0 0 0 7 7 *